revelation of Revelation

AN URGENT MESSAGE FOR THE CHURCH

VOLUME 5
THE FALL OF BABYLON AND THE CHURCH CORRUPT

*The Third Narrative
of
Revelation*

Rev 17:1-21:8

I0142123

The Naked Apostles
Phil and Colleen Livingston

Published by: The Naked Apostles

WAUCONDA, IL

Phil and Colleen Livingston/The Naked Apostles
304 Barrington Road
Wauconda, IL 60084
www.nakedapostles.org
email: info@nakedapostles.org

Ordering Information:
Quantity sales. Special discounts are available on quantity purchases by corporations, associations, and others. For details, contact via email or the address above.

revelation of Revelation, *An Urgent Message for the Church* Volume 5: The Fall of Babylon and the Church Corrupt/The Naked Apostles, Phil and Colleen Livingston.
2.2
ISBN-978-0-9960102-8-3

Table of Contents

This book is dedicated to those who partake in the first resurrection and hold true to their testimony of Jesus. May their testing prove faithful to their One and only first love, Jesus. Amen.

He who overcomes will inherit these things, and I will be his God and he will be My son.

— Revelation 21:7 New American Standard Bible

CHAPTER 1

The Woman on the Beast

NIV Rev 17:1 *One of the seven angels who had the seven bowls came and said to me, "Come, I will show you the punishment of the great prostitute, who sits on many waters.*

We just got finished with the previous narrative, Volume 4, The Main Characters of Revelation. It ended with the seven bowls of God's wrath poured out on Babylon in the world, of which this angel who spoke to John (above) in verse 1 was one of the executers of the bowls of wrath. Previous to that, in Volume 4, it had shown the harvest of the grapes which was the *Church Corrupt* being purified through the great tribulation. This angel who participated in the execution of the wrath of God against the world in the previous narrative is now beckoning John to show him the punishment of the great prostitute. The great prostitute is the *Church Corrupt* and the great tribulation is that "punishment" the angel wants to show John. In the last narrative the great tribulation was pictured as the crushing of the grapes in the wine press of God's wrath.

We can know this is a new narrative because where it begins is a repeat of what was covered in the previous narrative. However, this narrative, starting with the punishment of the great prostitute, is something which is more detailed and descriptive than it was in the last narrative. This woman on the beast is a prophetic picture worth a thousand words. The same thing that the great prostitute represents in this narrative was depicted as a cluster of grapes in the prophetic picture of the previous narrative. The previous narrative depicting the harvest of the *Church Corrupt* as clusters of grapes, crushed, was an overview of those circumstances.

This prophetic picture worth a thousand words of the woman riding the beast is a picture which gives us greater detail and is a closer look than the overview of the previous prophetic picture of grapes. All those things together make the point of this narrative, a story of its own. It is a story that does not have as its theme the main characters of Revelation as did the last narrative. It is the story of the utter and complete destruction of Babylon in both the Church and in the world. Included in this third narrative is the redemption of the *Church Corrupt* and the establishment of the Kingdom of God here on earth. This narrative is the story of the final stages of the execution of God's plan of both judgment and redemption.

> *NIV Rev 17:2* *With her the kings of the earth committed adultery and the inhabitants of the earth were intoxicated with the wine of her adulteries."*

This (above) is a statement which establishes a foundation for this story. By saying, "with her (the great prostitute) the kings of the earth committed adultery," it is telling us that the *Church Corrupt* is the great city that rules over the kings of the earth. Which means the *Church Corrupt* is the kingdom of Babylon. In fact, it is the seventh kingdom of Babylon which shockingly makes her the seventh head of the beast. This is all but impossible to believe, if it were not for Jesus revealing to us the contents of the scroll, and history reflecting exactly what we are told. It goes even further by telling us that the inhabitants of the earth were intoxicated (enamored, excited/inspired, devoted and in bondage to, even enriched) with the wine (spirit) of her adulteries. This confirms that the pope of the Catholic Church is the false prophet who seduces the people of the world. It is also exactly why Jesus personally admonished us, His Church, in the seven letters:

NIV Rev 2:19 *I know your deeds, your love and faith, your service and perseverance, and that you are now doing more than you did at first.*
NIV Rev 2:20 *Nevertheless, I have this against you: You tolerate that woman Jezebel, who calls herself a prophetess* (prophet: one who knows and interprets the divine will and purposes—the pope and Roman Catholic Church). *By her teaching she misleads my servants* (my Christians) *into sexual immorality and the eating of food sacrificed to idols.*
NIV Rev 2:21 *I have given her time to repent of her immorality, but she is unwilling.*

And again, Jesus warns at the last minute:

Amp Rev 18:4 *I then heard another voice from heaven saying, <u>Come out from her, my people, so</u>* <u>*that you may not share in her sins, neither participate in her plagues.*</u>
Amp Rev 18:5 *For her iniquities (her crimes and transgressions) are piled up as high as heaven, and God has remembered her wickedness and [her] crimes [and calls them up for settlement].*

NIV Rev 17:3a *Then the angel carried me away in the Spirit into a desert.*

Why is she said to be in a desert? This is because she, the *Church Corrupt*, is in a desolation—an absence of the presence of God guiding and protecting her. The remainder of the Church who was left behind is in a desert, or in a desolation during the time of the great tribulation. At the withdrawal of the two witnesses, the Holy Spirit, and the *Church Pure*, the *Church Corrupt* has been divorced and abandoned, left to her own devises to endure the great tribulation.

NIV Mt 25:28 " *'Take the talent from him and give it to the one who has the ten talents.*
NIV Mt 25:29 *For everyone who has will be given more, and he will have an abundance. <u>Whoever</u>* <u>*does not have, even what he has will be taken from him.*</u>
NIV Mt 25:30 <u>*And throw that worthless servant outside, into the darkness, where there will be*</u> <u>*weeping and gnashing of teeth.'*</u>

NIV Rev 3:16 <u>*So, because you are lukewarm—neither hot nor cold—I am about to spit you out of*</u> <u>*my mouth.*</u>
NIV Rev 3:17 *You say, 'I am rich; I have acquired wealth and do not need a thing.' But you do not realize that you are wretched, pitiful, poor, blind and naked.*
NIV Rev 3:18 *I counsel you to buy from me gold refined in the fire, so you can become rich; and white clothes to wear, so you can cover your shameful nakedness; and salve to put on your eyes, so you can see.*
NIV Rev 3:19 *Those whom I love I rebuke and discipline. So be earnest, and repent*

"I counsel you to buy from me gold refined in the fire, so you can become rich . . ." Since Jesus is saying, I am about to divorce you, He recommends this one thing you can do to win back your union with Him. That is to suffer the great tribulation while not coming off your testimony in Christ, not worshiping the beast, or taking his mark.

By saying, "and white clothes to wear so you can cover your shameful nakedness . . ." Jesus means, that when you die in the great tribulation and become disembodied (shamefully naked) sent to Hades, after you had not come off your testimony in Christ; had not worshiped the beast or taken his mark, you will have become refined as gold in the fire. Jesus will then clothe you with a celestial body (white [pure] clothes to wear), and you will become a celestial human, no longer disembodied in Hades, the realm of the dead.

She (the Church left behind) will have no power and can only overcome by being true to her profession of faith, not by opposing the government of the beast and antichrist. That would only amount to an exercise in futility.

NIV Rev 17:3b There I saw a woman sitting on a scarlet beast that was covered with blasphemous names and had seven heads and ten horns.

The beast is the same and is the prophetic characterization of both the Devil and the antichrist, who the Devil empowers. However, on this occasion, in this prophetic picture worth a thousand words, there is a difference. It is a scarlet beast the woman rides and controls with bit and bridle. Why scarlet? Scarlet not only is the color of blood, but represents blood, particularly in the Catholic Church. Later in a verse coming up we will read that the woman is dressed in scarlet and purple, however, here the beast is scarlet! It is because of its power being used for the killing of the Christians.

The time of Christianity starts at the release of the message of Christ when He walked the earth. The time of Christianity spans the sixth, seventh, and eighth kingdoms and kings of the beast. The sixth kingdom of the beast, the Roman Empire, was responsible for the persecution, torture, and death of many Christians. Jesus had warned about this in His letter to the church of Smyrna. He warned it would be ten days or 10 reigns of (10 different emperors) under which they would suffer persecution during the time of the Roman Empire. Each day represents the time of rule of an emperor of the Roman Empire. Therefore, 10 days equates to 10 different emperors and their tenure as the ruler of the Roman Empire.

After the tenth one passed, came Constantine. For all intents and purposes, from the time of Constantine forward, the Christians of the Roman Empire were no longer persecuted, tortured, or killed ever again for the rest of the empire's history. It was during the reign of Constantine that the death penalty for being a Christian was taken out of law.

During those ten reigns of emperors who persecuted the Christians, it is considered that there were times of outbreak which were not empire wide. Meaning, the outbreaks of persecution were contained within certain pockets of the empire and at different times during the reigns of those ten emperors. It was not a sustained persecution over the entire empire for 10 successive emperors. In fact, there were a handful of emperors in between some of those ten who did not persecute the Christians. Although some emperors didn't persecute the Christians, they neglected to remove the law-making death and the confiscation of their homes and possessions the penalty for being a Christian. That law-making Christianity illegal in the Roman Empire was unenforced by those emperors who did not persecute the Christians. Needless to say, when push came to shove, and a Christian found himself in court over any dispute, this was the law of the land which framed judgment. This kept an uneasy tension in the hearts of believers.

The sixth kingdom of the beast, the Roman Empire, is responsible for killing an estimated 2 million Christians.[1] There are estimates ranging from 50 million to as many as 150 million killed by the seventh kingdom of the beast, the Holy Roman Empire/Catholic Church of which the pope was and is in authority over. The number multiple historians have accredited the popery with having killed is 68 million.

The Roman Empire was responsible for millions of Christian deaths, but the Holy Roman Empire/the Catholic Church are responsible for tens of millions of Christian deaths. The eighth and final kingdom of the beast, of which the pope will wield a great influence over, will kill hundreds of millions of Christians. That is one third of the then Christian population. In fact, the numbers killed may exceed a billion depending on the population of Christians at that time. It is no small wonder that under the leadership of the woman (the Roman Catholic Church), who rides him, the beast, is covered with scarlet red—the blood of the saints!

Note: Because of the reported crimes of the Roman Catholic Church past (the Holy Roman Empire), history confirms on yet one more account that the Catholic Church is the great prostitute who rides the beast.

From the time of emperor Constantine until the fall of the Roman Empire and the emergence of the Holy Roman Empire, the *Church Corrupt* is being called by the Lord, a "prostitute." She has been prostituting herself to the sixth head of the beast and the kings of the world. She did so by looking to them as her power base, her protection, enforcement, and enrichment. By doing this the church is committing adultery on the Lord, her real husband, provider and protector. Likewise, the kings of the world interacting with the Church the way they do, they are committing adultery with the bride of another ... the bride of Christ.

> *NIV Rev 17:4a The woman was dressed in purple and scarlet,*

Purple and scarlet are the colors of the Roman Catholic Church and their leadership.

> *NIV Rev 17:4b and was glittering with gold, precious stones and pearls. She held a golden cup in her hand, filled with abominable things and the filth of her adulteries.*
>
> *NIV Rev 17:5 This title was written on her forehead:*
>
> *MYSTERY*
>
> *BABYLON THE GREAT*
>
> *THE MOTHER OF PROSTITUTES*
>
> *AND OF THE ABOMINATIONS OF THE EARTH.*

By her deeds the *Church Corrupt* has chosen to identify herself in the eyes of God as the names above. Gilgamesh by his deeds has identified himself in the eyes of God as "Nimrod." Nimrod means the one who rebels and the one who makes the people rebel (against Yahweh). That is what is on the forehead of Gilgamesh and is the title and name he is identified with. Just like Jesus has identified Himself as Christ or the Lamb of God by His deeds. Christ means the savior of the people. Likewise, someone who has killed would be labeled and called a murderer.

Again, by her deeds, these names are what the *Church Corrupt* has identified herself as in the eyes of God. Conversely, that is exactly who she is to God because of her deeds. She is Babylon! What a condemning commentary that she has already been judged by God as such. In addition, she has and will participate in the most abominable deeds possible on earth. Deeds so sacrilege and offensive to God that it has and will lead to desolations—the absence of the presence of God. His Spirit simply cannot be defiled by being hosted and embodied by the *Church Corrupt* forever.

Note: Before receiving interpretation of Revelation by the Lord and Holy Spirit, the authors would never consider calling the Catholic Church, Babylon. Nor could they believe the Catholic Church as being condemned or divorced from God. Never would it be in our imagination that the Roman Catholic Church is the seventh head and kingdom of the beast. However, here it is! The One who was found worthy has opened the scroll and has informed us (His Church) that this is the case. Likewise, the angel had to ask John why he was so astonished at this development. After the last word is given of the description of the prophetic picture of the *Church Corrupt,* the very next chapter starts with the punishment of the prostitute. When it does, all of heaven gives out a mighty shout of joy and triumph, worshiping God for her downfall during the great tribulation.

A spirit of denial made it hard to clear the fog from our eyes and come to terms with the fact that the Roman Catholic Church is evil, and it is them that all these bad things will happen to. Even more so, that all of heaven not only revels in its destruction, but has been waiting thousands of years for it to happen. At first consideration it is unimaginable to believe that the Roman Catholic Church knows where it is headed, and how it has gone over to the other side. It would be much easier to believe that they are blind to their standing with the Lord and are ignorant of what they are truly serving.

However, after understanding the book of Revelation, weighed against history, it is next to impossible to believe anything other than the highest levels of the Roman Catholic Church do know that they are leading the people into delusion and under the beast/antichrist in opposition to God. It takes great courage to see the pope in the Catholic Church in the light of truth. However, just as John was astonished when his eyes were opened to the truth about the beloved Church when Jesus told him of the future of the Church, we too must open our eyes to that same light of truth.

It is because of their adulteries against Him that the Lord punished the 10 tribes of Israel with the Assyrian Army, throwing them out of the Promised Land. Judah, who was saved from this fate, it was said later by the Lord, that they had become worse than Israel not taking their example as a warning. This resulted in Him using Babylon to punish and cast the Jews out of Jerusalem. Now, the Church has not only exceeded the sins and adulteries of Israel and Judah, but has become Babylon, the line of offspring of the Devil, and murderer of the saints. It cannot be ignored, the Lord who opened the scroll and informed us of its content, has told us even before it happened, the Roman Catholic Church is not His bride, but His enemy, Babylon.

In all this, the Lord gives benefit of doubt that the saints within the Roman Catholic Church are not on board with their secret agendas. He admonishes for them to get out before they share in her sin and in her punishment.

> *NIV Rev 17:6 I saw that the woman was drunk with the blood of the saints, the blood of those who bore testimony to Jesus.*
>
> *When I saw her, I was greatly astonished.*

From a number of historical accounts, the *Church Corrupt* has already been accredited with killing up to 60 million of its own, the lowest estimates being 40 million. Only God knows the real number. Is there any wonder why John is astonished? His beloved Church, which he has given his life for, just as his fellow apostles, will become this in the future after John has left this earth!

The *Church Corrupt* being drunk on the blood of the saints are referring to the many the Church killed in its history. Drunk, because the Roman Catholic Church was filled with a blood lust that they could not satisfy to kill those who they could not dominate.

Note: This is not the opinion of the authors, but history and the prophetic picture worth a thousand words that Jesus constructed for us, so that we might not be deceived. Likewise, it is how the Lord understands the Roman Catholic Church.

All this has taken place between now and reaching back to when Pope Leo III had revived what was to be called in later years, "the Holy Roman Empire." Since then, the Church became the 7th kingdom of the beast—Babylon.

In the future when the great tribulation comes, it will be the pope as the false prophet who will force all people of the world, to worship the beast under penalty of death. Most particularity, he will impose this requirement and enforce it by penalty of death, on all Christians. Many of which he is the pope and Holy See over (the Catholic Christians). However, the deaths which occur during the great tribulation perpetrated by the false prophet/pope is not the spilled blood verse 6 (above) is referring to. The great tribulation will be the punishment the Lord inflicts on the Church as a consequence for the Church becoming the 7th kingdom of the beast and its responsibility for the spilling of the blood the great prostitute is drunk on (the estimated 68 million).

Most of the Christians who are left behind at the rapture will agree that the two witnesses are not from God and want them stopped, even killed. Nor will they believe their message. However, it is very understandable to believe how those same Christians in massive numbers will finally defy the pope. They will be more than willing to die before conforming after their eyes are opened and they see the truth. The truth the two witnesses spoke saying, that the pope is the false prophet, he serves the beast and not the Lord. In addition, that he will kill everyone who refuses to worship the beast.

NIV Rev 17:7 Then the angel said to me: "Why are you astonished? I will explain to you the mystery of the woman and of the beast she rides, which has the seven heads and ten horns.

What the angel says to John (above) can only be compared to the moment he was shown how there was nobody alive or dead, in heaven or earth who was worthy to open the scroll. Then an elder came to him and said do not weep! See . . . In this occasion an angel says, "Why are you astonished? I will explain to you . . ." It is amazing the constitution John has in order to be brought to these truths and shocking realities. Daniel once said about the visions given him concerning the same time period:

NIV Da 8:26 "The vision of the evenings and mornings that has been given you is true, but seal up the vision, for it concerns the distant future."
NIV Da 8:27 I, Daniel, was exhausted and lay ill for several days. Then I got up and went about the king's business. I was appalled by the vision; it was beyond understanding.

We have here another case like with Eve and the Devil. Because of the one deed she did with him, they were bound together in enmity and you cannot tell the story of Eve any longer without telling the story of the Devil. It is like two enemies bound to each other by a short rope while in a knife fight to the death. Only one can survive. It is now the same with the *Church Corrupt* and the beast or antichrist. You cannot tell the story of the *Church Corrupt* without telling the story of the beast, and you cannot tell the story of the beast without telling the story of the *Church Corrupt*—they are bound together. This is why when telling John of the punishment of the great prostitute, the angel must explain to John the mystery of both the *Church Corrupt* and the beast.

WEB Rev 17:8a *The beast that you saw was, and is not; and is about to come up out of the abyss and to go into destruction.*

John was told by the angel that he would explain to him the mystery of the woman and of the beast she rides. He gives that explanation starting with the verse above 17:8 to the end of the chapter. That is 10 verses which are dedicated towards that explanation. Here is what's curious: 9 of those 10 verses tell about the beast she rides, not her. However, in explaining about the beast, the angel is explaining about the *Church Corrupt*. Because of their union with each other their stories become one. The *Church Corrupt* is so content with her status as the bride of Christ and her union with the beast that in arrogance she says:

Amp Rev 18:7b . . . *Since in her heart she boasts, I am not a widow; as a queen [on a throne] I sit, and I shall never see suffering or experience sorrow—*
Amp Rev 18:8 *So shall her plagues (afflictions, calamities) come thick upon her in a single day, pestilence and anguish and sorrow and famine; and she shall be utterly consumed (burned up with fire), for mighty is the Lord God Who judges her.*

Basically, the angel goes on to explain in those 10 verses that the prostitute empowers herself with the beast, and not with God. That actually became the state of the Church. Then, in order to divide His Church from the beast, God must put that hatred, that state of war, back between them as he had once established in the beginning, in the Garden. God accomplishes this by granting that the beast rises from the dead and making it the ordained destiny of the beast to turn on the great prostitute (the *Church Corrupt*) and destroy her. Why? It becomes obvious she will not turn on him, she is content with her place among the kings and leaders in the world.

It takes a drastic and harsh measure to break that union. She will not break up with the beast, so God puts it in the heart of the beast and of the false prophet to utterly destroy her in order to separate her from her union with the beast. It is the story of Hosea and Gomer. God made Gomer's lovers turn on her and despise her. In her desperation she came to her senses and decided she was better off going back to her husband.

NIV Hos 2:2 <u>"Rebuke your mother, rebuke her, for she is not my wife, and I am not her husband.</u> Let her remove the adulterous look from her face and the unfaithfulness from between her breasts.

NIV Hos 2:3 Otherwise I will strip her naked and make her as bare as on the day she was born; I will make her like a desert, turn her into a parched land, and slay her with thirst.

NIV Hos 2:4 <u>I will not show my love to her children, because they are the children of adultery.</u>

NIV Hos 2:5 <u>Their mother has been unfaithful and has conceived them in disgrace. She said, 'I will go after my lovers, who give me my food and my water, my wool and my linen, my oil and my drink.'</u>

NIV Hos 2:6 Therefore I will block her path with thornbushes; I will wall her in so that she cannot find her way.

NIV Hos 2:7 <u>She will chase after her lovers but not catch them; she will look for them but not find them. Then she will say, 'I will go back to my husband as at first, for then I was better off than now.'</u>

NIV Hos 2:8 She has not acknowledged that I was the one who gave her the grain, the new wine and oil, who lavished on her the silver and gold— which they used for Baal.

God divorces Israel as the illustration of Gomer and Hosea portrays. He abandons her, then puts a hedge around her causing her lovers to reject her and turn against her as well. This is an accurate portrayal of what happens during the great tribulation. The Lord spews the *Church Corrupt* out of His mouth (divorces) leaving her in a desolation, and also turns her lovers (the kings of the world) against her. Like Gomer, the *Church Corrupt* is hedged in while alone in her misery and rejection. It is then, during this time period of the great tribulation, the *Church Corrupt* will finally come to her senses and return to her first love—the Lord.

NIV Hos 2:9 "Therefore I will take away my grain when it ripens, and my new wine when it is ready. I will take back my wool and my linen, intended to cover her nakedness.

NIV Hos 2:10 <u>So now I will expose her lewdness before the eyes of her lovers; no one will take her out of my hands.</u>

NIV Hos 2:11 I will stop all her celebrations: her yearly festivals, her New Moons, her Sabbath days—all her appointed feasts.

NIV Hos 2:12 I will ruin her vines and her fig trees, which she said were her pay from her lovers; I will make them a thicket, and wild animals will devour them.

NIV Hos 2:13 I will punish her for the days she burned incense to the Baals; she decked herself with rings and jewelry, and went after her lovers, but me she forgot," declares the LORD.

NLT Hos 3:1 Then the LORD said to me, "Go and get your wife again. Bring her back to you and love her, even though she loves adultery. For the LORD still loves Israel even though the people have turned to other gods, offering them choice gifts."

NLT Hos 3:2 So I bought her back for fifteen pieces of silver and about five bushels of barley and a measure of wine.

NLT Hos 3:3 Then I said to her, "You must live in my house for many days and stop your prostitution. During this time, you will not have sexual intercourse with anyone, not even with me."

NLT Hos 3:4 This illustrates that Israel will be a long time without a king or prince, and without sacrifices, temple, priests, or even idols!

NLT Hos 3:5 But afterward the people will return to the LORD their God and to David's descendant, their king. They will come trembling in awe to the LORD, and they will receive his good gifts in the last days.

From the beginning in the Garden, the Lord put a division and hatred between the lines of offspring of the Devil and that of Eve's.

NIV Mt 10:32 "Whoever acknowledges me before men, I will also acknowledge him before my Father in heaven.

NIV Mt 10:33 But whoever disowns me before men, I will disown him before my Father in heaven.

NIV Mt 10:34 "Do not suppose that I have come to bring peace to the earth. I did not come to bring peace, but a sword.

NIV Mt 10:35 For I have come to turn " 'a man against his father, a daughter against her mother, a daughter-in-law against her mother-in-law—

NIV Mt 10:36 a man's enemies will be the members of his own household.'

NIV Mt 10:37 "Anyone who loves his father or mother more than me is not worthy of me; anyone who loves his son or daughter more than me is not worthy of me;

NIV Mt 10:38 and anyone who does not take his cross and follow me is not worthy of me.

NIV Mt 10:39 Whoever finds his life will lose it, and whoever loses his life for my sake will find it.

NIV Mt 10:40 "He who receives you receives me, and he who receives me receives the one who sent me.

NIV Mt 10:41 Anyone who receives a prophet because he is a prophet will receive a prophet's reward, and anyone who receives a righteous man because he is a righteous man will receive a righteous man's reward.

NIV Mt 10:42 And if anyone gives even a cup of cold water to one of these little ones because he is my disciple, I tell you the truth, he will certainly not lose his reward."

Jesus came to clarify and reestablish the chasm between the two lines of offspring. A chasm that He put in place at the beginning, in the Garden, in order to facilitate salvation. Jesus told us that we cannot serve two masters, we will love the one and hate the other. It is important to recognize that when Jesus came among us, He did not clarify the chasm by warring against the world with violence. He did so by letting the world have the world, then doing what the Father wanted done. However, since the beginning, the line of the offspring of Eve's has been hell bent at work, bridging the divine chasm between the two that the Lord had put in place. Bridging that gap was the demise of Israel, Judah, and now finally the Church who has shown itself no better than their Hebrew brothers, in fact much worse. The Church is the great prostitute!

In these contemporary times we find ourselves yielding all the more to the spirit of this world. We live in a time where it is the unbelievers, who do not know the Bible, that are interpreting the message in it for the believers.

NIV Ge 4:6 Then the LORD said to Cain, "Why are you angry? Why is your face downcast?
NIV Ge 4:7 If you do what is right, will you not be accepted? But if you do not do what is right, sin is crouching at your door; it desires to have you, but you must master it."

We live in a time that the world demands we give acceptance without conformity, not only accepting the sinner, but also his sin. Although blanket acceptance and forgiveness may achieve the appearance of peace, in reality it destroys the gap which shows us as the Lord's offspring, then divides us from Him. Blanket acceptance and forgiveness first blurs, then erodes the boundaries until we are one with the world. We forever end up relating down to the world instead of requiring it to relate up to us. This is defined as codependence and enabling.

If there will be peace between the two, it will not be because the world will relate up and do what is right in the eyes of God. They are unwilling to yield just as Cain was not. He tried to solve the problem by killing his brother and eliminating the other line of offspring just as the false prophet and the beast will do. This is a solution which does not require conformity.

The Church must get it in their heads that peace, unity, and acceptance is not the most important thing to achieve in this world among humanity. However, those of the religion of Cain and delusional Christians believe it is. That chasm, and enmity was put there by God Himself in order to achieve the most important thing; salvation for those who would conform to God in order to be accepted by Him. It is the religion of Cain, the philosophy of harmony through acceptance without conformity—to coexist—that will bring the end and a final conflict between God and humanity. The hope of the world is the antichrist Nimrod who promised, "Do as you will, and I will protect you from Yahweh." He is the self-proclaimed savior and champion for the religion of Cain; to gain acceptance without conformity.

Our Christian/Biblical beliefs about right and wrong not only are clear, but are from the One true God. That is, even if the rest of the world doesn't believe it and instead holds as true some ideas which are false to the truth. It is ironic that the unbelievers who do not read the Bible tell us that we are supposed to love, forgive, and accept them for who they are in their sin. We are told by them we act against the Bible if we don't, and that we are not real Christians. Here's the bad part; we believe them, we who do read the Bible. All this is not to say that we do not treat the world with human dignity, and respect, we do and are called to do so in order to woo them into conformity to God.

There are many, even countless, spiritual influences in the universe, however, we must remember it was only to One individual out of all in heaven or in earth that God revealed His plan for judgment and redemption. It is only that One individual who was found worthy and makes known to humanity that plan which was revealed to Him alone. He alone is the way, the truth, and the life. Nevertheless, there is a huge and powerful movement rising up in the Church today that for the sake of peace, are destroying the enmity between the two different lines of offspring, while subscribing to the religion of Cain.

What an incredibly pitiful commentary against the Church that the Lord cannot open up the eyes of His own bride. He cannot bring her to her senses so that she stops her adultery and turns away from her union with the world. After trying everything, it proves effective to cause the world to reject her and push her away with great violence in order to separate her from them. He has to count on the hatred of the world to push her away, instead of counting on her love to return to His arms. Is it any clearer why He has to put His Church through the great tribulation?

Amp Rev 7:9 After this I looked and a vast host appeared which no one could count, [gathered out] of every nation, from all tribes and peoples and languages. These stood before the throne and before the Lamb; they were attired in white robes, with palm branches in their hands.
Amp Rev 7:10 In loud voice they cried, saying, [Our] salvation is due to our God, Who is seated on the throne, and to the Lamb [to Them we owe our deliverance]!
Amp Rev 7:11 And all the angels were standing round the throne and round the elders [of the heavenly Sanhedrin] and the four living creatures, and they fell prostrate before the throne and worshiped God.
Amp Rev 7:12 Amen! (So be it!) they cried. Blessing and glory and majesty and splendor and wisdom and thanks and honor and power and might [be ascribed] to our God to the ages and ages (forever and ever, throughout the eternities of the eternities)! Amen! (So be it!)

However, once this great multitude who suffer from this great violence are set free from their bondage to the world, we read in Revelation (above) how grateful they are that in the Lord's wisdom He took these measures to save them.

> *WEB Rev 17:8b Those who dwell on the earth and whose names have not been written in the book of life from the foundation of the world will marvel when they see that the beast was, and is not (now), and shall be present (again).*

Those whose names are written in the book of life have been told by Jesus (who is the spirit of prophecy) the plan of judgment and redemption, the contents of the scroll with seven seals. They know that the beast and antichrist is someone who escapes the Abyss, which is the bottomless pit in Hades, the realm of the dead and will come back to life in a body not constructed by God but by human hands. Those whose names are written in the book of life, also know that he has a short time granted by God in order to serve the purposes of God. He then afterwards will be thrown alive into the lake of fire suffering the second and eternal death.

Those whose names are not written in the book of life, they do not believe and do not know the plan of God as revealed by the Lord. It says here that they will be astonished, and marvel at this turn of events. Everyone, both alive and dead from the beginning of the world, will be taken back. That is even if they do know what is written in the Bible because they will not believe or make sense of what it says. Only the Spirit of prophecy can make people understand and let it witness deep within them that these things will come to pass and why. It will be only them whose names are written in the book of life that will not be surprised but will actually be found waiting for it when it transpires. They will, in turn, know what to do to escape these times.

> *WEB Rev 17:9* *Here is the mind that has wisdom.* *The seven heads are seven mountains* (hills) *on* *which the woman sits.*

The capitol or center of its rule and the government of an empire is the head of that empire. Since its inception Rome has always been known as the city on seven hills. That is why, when Rome was sacked, and its government gave way to its conquerors, it was said it had suffered a fatal head wound. The head and center of rule of any of the seven kingdoms of the beast while they are in power is the great city of Babylon that rules the kings of the earth. Rome, the city on seven hills, is the great city that rules the kings of the earth during the time of the Roman Empire (the sixth kingdom of the beast), and when John received this prophecy.

What verse 9 tells us is intended to give a clue which identifies who the great prostitute is; that is, when that time comes in the future of when John received this prophecy. What we are being told here is that the capitol or center of the government of the great prostitute is (or will be) seated in Rome. During her time of prostituting herself to Babylon, it was the Roman Empire that she did so with, which Rome was the head of. Rome is the head of the beast during the Roman Empire and was who she prostituted herself to until it was sacked (its head was severed from its empire bringing to its end).

Next, Rome becomes where the great prostitute's government is seated. Rome is the head of both the sixth and now the seventh kingdom of the beast. Only the Roman Catholic Church fits these criteria, because its headquarters is in the city of Rome causing Rome to continue to be the great city of Babylon who rules the kings of the earth.

> *WEB Rev 17:10* *They are seven kings. Five have fallen, the one is, the other has not yet come. When he* *comes, he must continue a little while.*

In Micah, it was written that there would be seven shepherds/kings and kingdoms of Babylon. That agrees with verse 10 (above). However, verse 10 also tells us where we are at in the timeline of God's plan as of the time John received this prophecy. Five of the seven kings and kingdoms of Babylon have come and gone. John is told, "one is." That would mean John received this prophecy during the time of the sixth king and kingdom of the beast. That would be the Roman Empire which history informs us. John is told by the angel that the other, or the last of the seven kings and kingdoms will come in the future of him receiving this prophecy.

It has already been established that the seventh king and kingdom is the pope and the Holy Roman Empire, AKA, the Roman Catholic Church. In this first vision of this third narrative we are getting ahead of what it is revealing by identifying the Roman Catholic Church as the seventh king and kingdom. However, because of the prophetic picture of the great prostitute, she is identified as the *Church Corrupt*. The angel adds that when the Roman Catholic Church (the seventh king and kingdom of the beast) comes into its power, it "must" remain for a little while.

Many believe this to mean the seventh king will have his kingdom for only a short time. To say he "must continue a little while" has a twofold prophetic meaning. "A little while," has a meaning for each of the two horns the king of the seventh kingdom of the beast possesses. The first prophetic meaning for one of the horns of power is not saying it will only be for a short time. But instead by saying that, it is inferring that he will, by the decree of God, continue in his time of power for an extended or designated amount of time—he must continue for a little while . . . God has a perfect time and arrangements for when the Lord will crush the head of the Devil and his offspring. The seventh king and kingdom is the last of time God had ordained to the beast. The next king of Babylon will be the beast himself—the eighth king. As such, the seventh king and kingdom must continue until the time is right.

That time will be:
- After the last seven of the 70-7's has passed
- After the Church Age is complete
- After the testimony of Christ (the Gospel) has been spread to every corner of the globe
- After the testimony of the Lord is completed by being released through the ministry of the two witnesses
- After the beast rises from the dead and is on the Lord's holy mountain where he must (according to the plan and decree of God) be crushed

Until all these things and more align themselves, converging at the exact right point in time, the seventh king and kingdom "must" continue (for a little while).

The second meaning of that verse, which applies to the second horn of power (like a lamb), is that this same king of the seventh kingdom of the beast will transition into the false prophet for the beast. When he comes into that role and raises the beast from the dead, he "must" be in power during that time to do so according to God's decree. His time as the false prophet for the beast when the beast finally rules the entire globe, is the pinnacle of the false prophet's ordained destiny. However, that time will indeed be short lived. Seven years to be exact.

Nevertheless, we know by both history, weighed against this verse, that we (in these contemporary times) live in the time of the seventh king and kingdom of the beast. That is a witness to the fact that time is short, and the end will definitely come soon.

WEB Rev 17:11 The beast that was, and is not (now), is himself also an eighth, and is of the seven; and he goes to destruction.

The beast is:

The antichrist who would save the people of the world from Yahweh so that they can do as they will;

The Assyrian who was the first to conquer territories not his own, enslave the people and build great urban centers;

Nimrod who rebelled against God and incited the people to do likewise, and who was the first king and founder of Babylon;

The seed of Ham and his wife who survived and came out of the flood waters to continue the corrupted line of the offspring of the Devil, and whose ordained destiny and legacy it is for his kingdom to continue unbroken. A kingdom ordained by God to be continuous, but with seven different faces lasting until the end. Ending when the enmity between the two lines of offspring have their final contest for domination of the world;

The (soulless) **beast** who is demonically led, was once alive, but is now dead. He will in the future come back to life, and then be thrown alive into the lake of fire for eternity. That is, after he has had his seven years to finally fulfill his destiny to rule the entire globe and persecute the saints.

This individual in verse 11 (above) is Nimrod who is the Assyrian, antichrist, the beast with seven heads, and the first king and founder of Babylon. In order to fulfill prophecy, he will come back from the dead in order to finally rule the entire globe and be defeated by the Lord in Jerusalem, which had been granted him by God. When his time comes to rule the earth, it will be when his six other heads have had their ordained time. It is then that he will return as an eighth king, however, he was already one of the seven, he was the founder. When his time has served the purposes of the Lord in His plan of redemption, the risen Nimrod will receive judgment with his entire kingdom coming to his ruin for 3-1/2 years ending with Armageddon. That is when he will finally go to his destruction and suffer his second death by being thrown alive in the lake of fire for eternity.

> WEB Rev 17:12 *The ten horns that you saw are ten kings who have received no kingdom as yet, but they receive authority as kings, with the beast, for one hour.* [13] *These have one mind* (purpose), *and they give their power and authority to the beast*

When the risen Nimrod comes to his grand finale and has his global kingdom, God has decreed that Nimrod will divide up the globe and give authority to 10 kings. Like the false prophet, the 10 kings will have but one purpose, and that is to gain such power by committing to give everything to serve the beast. They do not care the cost, nor that it is only for a short time, but sell their souls to have that ultimate power. They lust for ultimate power out from under every authority, especially that of God's. That is the boast and promise of Nimrod, to free them from the authority and consequences of the Creator of the universe. Including that he seeks to fight God to the death and kill Him once and for all.

> WEB Rev 17:14 *These* (ten kings) *will war against the Lamb, and the Lamb will overcome them, for he is Lord of lords, and King of kings, and those who are with him are called chosen and faithful."*

Verse 14 (above) is a concluding statement about the ten kings. It tells us of the end of them. When it says they will war against the Lamb, that war begins with the killing of all the saints, the great tribulation. The ten kings will be instrumental, even indispensable when it comes to seeking out, imprisoning, and killing the Christians. Their warring against the Lamb will end with them gathering the people of the globe together to fight the Lord at the battle of Armageddon. The end of it all? The Lord will not only triumph with His chosen and faithful but will crush their power so thoroughly that there will be nothing left to rise up out of the ashes.

The purpose of what the angel wanted to reveal to John was these two things:

1) *NIV Rev 17:1* ... *I will show you the punishment of the great prostitute, who sits on many waters.*

2) *NIV Rev 17:7* ... *I will explain to you the mystery of* A) *the woman* B) *and of the beast she rides,* *which has* C) *the seven heads* D) *and ten horns*

Now that the angel made a concluding statement about the nature of the ten kings, in the verses to come (below) he gives John some details which tie the beast, his seven heads, and his ten horns to the woman who rides the beast.

> *WEB Rev 17:15* *He said to me, "The waters which you saw, where the prostitute sits, are peoples, multitudes, nations, and languages.*

Where the prostitute sits is where her seat of power is. The angel explains that the waters are peoples, multitudes, nations and languages. If she sits on these "many waters," it means that she sits in authority over those peoples, multitudes, nations and languages. This helps us understand that it is the time for the end, because the Gospel has been preached all around the world (multitudes, nations and languages).

NIV Ac 1:8 *But you will receive power when the Holy Spirit comes on you; and you will be my witnesses in Jerusalem, and in all Judea and Samaria, and to the ends of the earth."*
Amp Mt 28:18 *Jesus approached and, breaking the silence, said to them, All authority (all power of rule) in heaven and on earth has been given to Me.*
Amp Mt 28:19 *Go then and make disciples of all the nations, baptizing them into the name of the Father and of the Son and of the Holy Spirit,*
Amp Mt 28:20 *Teaching them to observe everything that I have commanded you, and behold, I am with you all the days (perpetually, uniformly, and on every occasion), to the [very] close and consummation of the age.*
NLT Mt 24:14 *And the Good News about the Kingdom will be preached throughout the whole world, so that all nations will hear it; and then, finally, the end will come.*

The fact that the woman—the Church—has her seat of authority over peoples, multitudes, nations and languages, means the great commission has been fulfilled. Furthermore, the Church Age in its sevenness has finished its time, and now finally the end can come. The house of the wedding feast is full (Lk 14:23), and now it is finally time for the harvest. The harvesters can now separate the darnel from the wheat with no danger of uprooting the wheat while doing so (Mt 13:24-30).

It is not good that the woman rides the beast because it means she empowers herself with the power of the beast. She has prostituted herself with the beast and the kings of the earth, and is in spiritual adultery, unfaithful to the Lord.

The wheat will be gathered into His barn (raptured), and the darnel will be thrown into the fire of the great tribulation. The purpose is not to destroy them, but to purify them. To consume, as fire does, everything in their life which binds them in union with Babylon will be destroyed—consumed by fire.

NLT 1Co 3:11 For no one can lay any other foundation than the one we already have—Jesus Christ.
NLT 1Co 3:12 Now anyone who builds on that foundation may use gold, silver, jewels, wood, hay, or straw.
NLT 1Co 3:13 But there is going to come a time of testing at the judgment day to see what kind of work each builder has done. Everyone's work will be put through the fire to see whether or not it keeps its value.
NLT 1Co 3:14 If the work survives the fire, that builder will receive a reward.
NLT 1Co 3:15 But if the work is burned up, the builder will suffer great loss. The builders themselves will be saved, but like someone escaping through a wall of flames.
NLT 1Co 3:16 Don't you realize that all of you together are the temple of God and that the Spirit of God lives in you?
NLT 1Co 3:17 God will bring ruin upon anyone who ruins this temple. For God's temple is holy, and you Christians are that temple.
NLT 1Co 3:18 Stop fooling yourselves. If you think you are wise by this world's standards, you will have to become a fool so you can become wise by God's standards.

> *WEB Rev 17:16 The ten horns which you saw, and the beast, these will hate the prostitute, and will make her desolate, and will make her naked, and will eat her flesh, and will burn her utterly with fire. 17 For God has put in their hearts to do what he has in mind, and to be of one mind, and to give their kingdom to the beast, until the words of God should be accomplished.*

Having framed and explained the relationship between the woman and the beast she rides, the angel now reveals the mystery of God's plan (starting with verse 16 above). It is to use the 10 kings and the beast to separate the woman from them by putting it in their hearts to reject, hate, and destroy her. If only the *Church Corrupt* had preserved that chasm by honoring the enmity the Lord put between the lines of offspring. The Lord had decreed and established that chasm in both the Garden and by the sword of division Jesus put in place through His death on the cross (Mt: 10:32-39).

To strip her naked is to kill the people and cause them to be "shamefully naked." In other words, to be disembodied and sent to Hades. To eat her flesh, is to take everything from her, her stature, influence, wealth, buildings and homes. To burn her utterly with fire is to, by the power they have, consume everything the *Church Corrupt* and her people have. Suddenly, they will have nothing, and nothing that makes them one with the world.

This is God's doing! It says He put it in their hearts to hate her and destroy her and in doing so accomplish what He has in mind for them. God has also put in their hearts to be of one mind in this obsession and passion to destroy the *Church Corrupt*. In the beginning, God divided their hearts so there would be seven different heads and kingdoms of the beast which served to slow down the ability of Babylon to conquer and rule the entire world. However, now, God puts it in their hearts to be in perfect unity in their hatred and desire to kill the *Church Corrupt*. As a result, no one in the world will oppose or object to the genocide of the Christians.

They will:
- want to save the whales
- fight for the right to abort babies
- the collective world will (continue to) protest the trapping of animals for their fur
- the collective world will unite in calling it murder, forcing the animal sacrifices to stop in the temple of God, giving animals more reverence than human beings;
- the collective world will be appalled and stop the harvesting of trees to save them, stop using fossil fuels
- In anger and with murder in their hearts for the sake of global peace accept and give rights to every kind of perversion and antisocial behavior which is in defiance to God's order, taking rights away from the righteous

However, in all this, the collective world will be of one heart to genocide the Christians. God has put it in their hearts to do so. God will give the people of this world the power and authority to do it until the very moment His purposes have been served. Then, as we have learned in other places, it will suddenly and abruptly stop with the tables suddenly turned against them.

WEB Rev 17:18 The woman whom you saw is the great city, which reigns over the kings of the earth."

It is of utmost importance to recognize that it is the Roman Catholic Church in Rome who has become the great city (of Babylon) who rules the kings of the world. The pope is the seventh head and the Roman Catholic Church is the seventh kingdom of the beast.

What makes a city the "great city" (according to Biblical usage) is that it is the capitol of the reigning kingdom of Babylon. It is identified as the great city because it is from that city that the head of the kingdom rules from. From the great city (of Babylon) the kings of the earth are ruled. We were told a few verses ago that the woman who rides the beast sits on the (city of) seven hills, which is Rome. What this means is the woman is headquartered in Rome.

This information goes far in identifying the woman as the Roman Catholic Church who is headquartered in Rome, the city of seven hills. As the Roman Catholic Church became the seventh head of the beast, and her head or headquarters is in Rome, Rome became the great city, again. Verse 18 (above) says straight up that the woman is the great city that reigns over the kings of the earth. This final statement tells us she has gone from prostituting herself to Babylon, to becoming Babylon. One of the two witnesses who come at the end verify the great city is the capitol of Babylon.

NLT Rev 14:8 ... "Babylon is fallen—that great city is fallen ... "

Therefore, the great city is Babylon, and Babylon is the Roman Catholic Church (the *Church Corrupt),* and the Roman Catholic Church is the great prostitute who rides the beast.

Rome was the great city for the kingdom of the sixth head of the beast, the Roman Empire. The Roman Empire and its emperor were the sixth kingdom and king of whom the angel told John, "is." It was preceded by the five which "had fallen." Concerning the seventh kingdom and king, John was told he, "is to come" and when he does, "he would remain a little while." Now we are told here in verse 18 (above) that the seventh head/king and kingdom is the woman who rides the beast. It tells us that by saying the woman is the great city. The pope and Roman Catholic Church (the Holy Roman Empire) is that seventh king and kingdom who are headquartered in Rome and are the great city of Babylon who rules the kings of the world. As an additional confirmation, the colors of the leadership of the Catholic Church are purple and scarlet, which also identifies the woman who rides the beast as the pope and the Roman Catholic Church (Rev 17:4a).

The Eastern Roman Empire along with its Eastern Orthodox Catholic Church was established by Constantine and by virtue of this, the Eastern Orthodox Church has also prostituted herself to the kings of the world. In fact, even the reformed church of Protestants and Lutherans who divided from the great prostitute while recognizing her sin, eventually went the same way as the Roman Church. Likewise are the reformed churches whose kings have assumed the headship of the church in their nation.

They all have prostituted themselves with the kings of the world, while fighting for control of territories, and nations against the Roman Catholic Church. As a result, they too are the *Church Corrupt* and will be destroyed during the great tribulation. Again, although the Eastern Orthodox Church and the reformed churches have become corrupt as well, it is the Roman Catholic Church which has the distinction of being the seventh head (the seventh king and kingdom) of the beast.

Notes

[1] *Ancient Christian Martyrdom.* Retrieved June 2018, from *Dallas Baptist University:* *http://www3.dbu.edu/mitchell/anceint_christian_martyrdom.htm*

CHAPTER 2

The Fall of Babylon

WEB Rev 18:1 After these things, I saw another angel coming down out of the sky, having great authority. The earth was illuminated with his glory. ² He cried with a mighty voice, saying, "Fallen, fallen is Babylon the great, and she has become a habitation of demons, a prison of every unclean spirit, and a prison of every unclean and hateful bird!

When John says, "after these things," he is referring to after receiving from the one angel the visions and explanations given him about the woman who rides the beast, her punishment, the beast, his seven heads, and his ten horns. Then John tells us that he saw another angel coming down. It's important to take note of the unfolding of these visions because they say as much as the words do.

The first angel showed John that the woman (the Roman Catholic Church) had originally prostituted herself to the beast for enrichment, protection, and power. Then the angel closes his explanation with the very last words which say the woman/prostitute/the Roman Catholic Church is the great city who rules the kings of the earth. This is a shocking development! Mostly because on the heels of saying the church in Rome is the great city, another angel comes down and announces, fallen, fallen is Babylon the great, and that she has become a habitation of demons, a prison of every unclean spirit, and a prison of every unclean and hateful bird!

Again, the first angel had said among other things, "Come, I will show you the punishment of the great prostitute." However, in all that he framed and gave background to, he did not, in fact, show the punishment of the great prostitute as of his last statement calling her the great city. The very first occasion which has to do with John being shown punishment, is when this next angel swoops down and proclaims, "Fallen, fallen is Babylon the great!" The preceding statement declared the *Church Corrupt* as the great city, Babylon. What this means is that the destruction of Babylon is the destruction of the great prostitute who rides the beast! Babylon falling is the great tribulation! The *Church Corrupt* will be destroyed so thoroughly that it will never rise again. The smoke of her burning rises from eternities to eternities (Amp Rev 19:3).

The next thing to take note of is that the angel said, "fallen, fallen is Babylon . . ." In Rev 8:3 there was an angel who came down saying "woe, woe, woe, to those who dwell on the earth." The reason he said "woe" three times is because there were three "woes" the inhabitants of the earth would suffer. There is, likewise, a reason why on this occasion this angel says fallen twice ("fallen, fallen is Babylon . . ."). That reason is because there are two elements of Babylon which fall. Those two elements fall in quick succession to each other. Those two elements are 1) Babylon in the Church, and 2) Babylon in the world.

This is the precise reason that although the sixth and seventh seals are released together and are the release of the same thing, they are together, the release of the punishment of Babylon. The emphasis on the sixth seal is the punishment of Babylon in the *Church Corrupt*. Whereas, the emphasis on the seventh seal is the punishment of Babylon in the world. They are destroyed one at a time in quick succession to each other. Babylon in the world, you might say, flourishes during the destruction of Babylon in the Church. In fact, it is Babylon in the world God uses, even puts it in their hearts and empowers them to punish Babylon in the Church.

Is that cruel? No, but necessary. The Lord told us through Hosea this is the only way He can woo us back. He could not cause Gomer to turn away from chasing her lovers believing that she needed them. But He could cause her lovers to despise her, turn on her, and drive her away. Then, and only then, did she finally get it into her heart while truly believing she was better off with her husband. The *Church Corrupt* wants to be the Lord's bride by profession only, however, she lusts after and is faithful to the powers of this world and the beast. When He puts it in the heart of the beast, the false prophet, and the ten horns to hate the Church, the *Church Corrupt* will then realize, while truly believing in her heart, that she is better off with her first love, the Lord.

In contrast to that, it is nature, the supernatural, supernatural beings, and finally the Lord Himself who are the instruments of destruction against Babylon in the world. However, to be clear, there are not two Babylons, there is only one beast and his Babylon. There are two elements but there is only one Babylon. There may be 50 states in the United States of America, but there is only one United States of America. The only difference between the two elements of Babylon, is that one is salvaged by being forcibly torn away from the other. That element of Babylon becomes the great multitude of heaven because it lets itself be rejected and separated from union with the spirit and power of Babylon, and thereby returning to their first love—Jesus. The other element of Babylon, will, with its last and dying breath, curse God and defy Him.

NLT Rev 18:2 ... *She has become the hideout of demons and evil spirits, a nest for filthy buzzards, and a den for dreadful beasts.*

The fall of Babylon starting with 18:1 is focused on the first "fallen." It is both the great tribulation and punishment of Babylon in the Church—the woman on the beast. That makes it the sixth seal. The seventh seal is broken simultaneously, but there is a half hour of silence (3-1/2 years) before the heavenly host pours out wrath on Babylon in the world—the beast she rides.

The above underlined summary of the fallen Church is a frightening and morbid look at her condition in the world after the great tribulation and the harvest of the grapes. If anyone has any love for the Church or for the people in it and takes a moment to let these words create a picture in their mind, they won't be able to stop themselves from sobbing. It happens as it was foretold:

WEB Rev 17:16 ... *these will hate the prostitute, and will make her desolate, and will make her naked, and will eat her flesh, and will burn her utterly with fire.*

What a haunting and vivid picture! Imagine the opulent Catholic cathedrals of Europe looted and burnt out and the smoke of them rising up to the heavens. No roofs as if they were bombed out, no windows or doors for they have been broken. The inside littered with the dead, young, old, men, women, and children. So much carnage you can't walk on the floor without stepping on the bodies. The stench of their decaying bodies can be smelled for miles. You can see the ghostly demons shifting about in the corner of your eyes, giving chills of fear running up your spine, while hearing the screams that linger even after the dead fell silent. No one cares to give them a decent burial, but all simply avoid going near, or stand afar while mocking or stare in astonishment at the Church, who thought they were above reproach. Birds and scavengers of every kind are feasting on their bodies, the only things which move about. Scavenger beasts hide among the rubble. It is a picture of death and decay, almost if without color but gray, dingy, and lifeless.

This is not a Steven King novel, or a horror movie, this is what the Lord said will become of us when we do not take this message seriously and come out of her to be snatched up before the great tribulation. What the Lord says here will happen!

> *NIV Rev 18:3 For all the nations have drunk the maddening wine of her adulteries.*
>
> *The kings of the earth committed adultery with her,*
>
> *and the merchants of the earth grew rich from her excessive luxuries."*

Verses 18:1-2 (above) is a summary statement about the punishment of the woman who rides the beast which includes the punishment of the beast she rides. Starting with verse 3 (immediately above), we learn of the circumstances surrounding her punishment.

To this day, visitors are in awe of the beauty and wealth of the Vatican and its buildings. Because of the pure opulence of the Roman Catholic Church and its buildings, the merchants of the earth did indeed grow rich with the Roman Catholic Church as their best customer.

The maddening wine of wrath:

NIV Isa 51:17 Awake, awake! Rise up, O Jerusalem, you who have drunk from the hand of the LORD the cup of his wrath, you who have drained to its dregs the goblet that makes men stagger.
NIV Isa 51:18 Of all the sons she bore there was none to guide her; of all the sons she reared there was none to take her by the hand.
NIV Isa 51:19 These double calamities have come upon you—who can comfort you?—ruin and destruction, famine and sword—who can console you?
NIV Isa 51:20 Your sons have fainted; they lie at the head of every street, like antelope caught in a net. They are filled with the wrath of the LORD and the rebuke of your God.

Revelation 18:3 (above) tells us:

NRSV Rev 18:3 *For all the nations have drunk of the wine of the wrath of her fornication, and the kings of the earth have committed fornication with her, and the merchants of the earth have grown rich from the power of her luxury.*

"Her" is Babylon and this verse 3 (above) reaches back to describe all seven heads (kings and kingdoms) of the beast. The tip of the iceberg is what we behold with its mass being so much greater below the surface, however, the tip above the surface is one and the same as the iceberg below. What it says is true for all of Babylon reaching back through time to the beginning, to Nimrod the first king and founder of Babylon. Although "her" is Babylon, in this verse "her" and the wrath of her maddening wine is referring to the visible and relevant tip of the iceberg, the Roman Catholic Church and seventh kingdom of Babylon.

When the two witnesses spoke giving their testimony in the previous narrative, it was them who said that she had made all the nations drink the wine of the wrath of her fornication. It was one of the two witness in verse 18:1 whose splendor made the earth grow bright with the light of their testimony and the power of their authority:

NRSV Rev 14:8 *Then another angel, a second, followed* (the second of the two witnesses), *saying, "Fallen, fallen is Babylon the great!* <u>*She has made all nations drink of the wine of the wrath of her fornication.*</u>*"*

How did she make the nations drink of the wine of the wrath of her fornication? The answer is that it was by the same means that she (the church and little horn) was able to revive the Roman Empire and become an authority over all of Rome's conquerors, without a shot fired in force. That little horn which is the Roman Catholic Church has the eyes making him a prophet and a boastful mouth speaking blasphemies. Indeed, the popery and Roman Catholic Church are the false prophet. It was and is through manipulation, lies and deceit in a most prideful and boastful way that they had fashioned their position in the world. The seat of the pope claims God's total spiritual authority on earth. That it is him, the pope, who claims that the people are obliged to be loyal to, and that he has the absolute authority on earth which should be obeyed above all powers and authority. This extends even to include a supremacy over the scriptures and interpretation of them.

Below is an account of a conflict of power between the pope and the emperor of the Holy Roman Empire revealing how the, then pope, wielded the seducing power of his blasphemous boast.

Pope Gregory VII and King Henry IV

Conflicts between the medieval Christian church, led by the Pope, and nations, ruled by kings, occurred throughout the Middle Ages. One great clash between a pope and a king took place between Pope Gregory VII and King Henry IV of the Holy Roman Empire. Henry was very young when he became king. As early as the age of fifteen, Henry moved to increase his power over clergy in the Holy Roman Empire. Eventually Henry's actions brought him into conflict with Pope Gregory VII who was one of the great leaders of the Medieval Church. Pope Gregory was both devout and clever. He worked to bring spiritual reform to the church by increasing the power and authority of the popes. Gregory believed that the church was the supreme authority on earth; he felt that rulers and ordinary people alike were all subject to the will of the church and its pope. He did not hesitate to use the terrible punishment of excommunication as a way to resolve conflicts of church and state. The conflict between Henry IV and Gregory VII concerned the question of who got to appoint local church officials. Henry believed that, as king, he had the right to appoint the bishops of the German church. This was known as lay investiture. Pope Gregory, on the other hand, angrily opposed this idea because he wanted the power for himself. He responded to the emperor's attempts to name new bishops by excommunicating Henry. In addition, Gregory used an interdict to released the emperor's subjects from their feudal obligations of loyalty to their leader. Fearing the rebellion of his vassals, Henry sought the Pope's mercy. During the harsh winter of 1077, Henry and his servants made a long and dangerous journey through the snowy mountains of northern Italy to meet the Pope. They met in a small town called Canossa in the mountains of northern Italy. Then when he arrived, the Pope made the humiliated Henry wait in the bitter cold for three days before finally agreeing to see him. Contemporary accounts report that when Henry was finally permitted to enter the gates, he walked barefoot through the snow and knelt at the feet of the pope to beg forgiveness. As a result, the Pope revoked Henry's excommunication. [2]

It was not by force of arms, but by blasphemous and false boasts that the pope was able to influence and impose his dominance on the king of both the nation of Germany and the Holy Roman Empire. Not only was the king forced to be subject to the pope, but the citizens of Germany and all of Christian Europe under the Holy Roman Empire were ordered by the pope that they had no obligation or owed no loyalty to the king of both Germany and the Holy Roman Empire. This was obviously a real power that he had over the hearts and minds of the people of Christian Europe. Otherwise it would not have impressed King Henry IV in the least, however, it caused him to degrade and humiliate himself, then on his knees, beg the pope to give him reprieve.

All this without a shot fired in anger! It was through lies, deception, and blasphemous boasts that the popery employed to create his seat of power over the kings and people of the earth, claiming spiritual authority he did not have. It was not by the will of God nor the power of His Holy Spirit, but by the lust for power of the pope. It was by the authority and power of the beast that this great wave of delusion could seduce, hypnotize, and dominate both the kings and people of the earth! A power Pope Leo III sold his soul to attain.

How do we know this is not by the power of the Holy Spirit?

NIV Jn 18:33 Pilate then went back inside the palace, summoned Jesus and asked him, "Are you the king of the Jews?"
NIV Jn 18:34 "Is that your own idea," Jesus asked, "or did others talk to you about me?"
NIV Jn 18:35 "Am I a Jew?" Pilate replied. "It was your people and your chief priests who handed you over to me. What is it you have done?"
NIV Jn 18:36 Jesus said, "My kingdom is not of this world. If it were, my servants would fight to prevent my arrest by the Jews. But now my kingdom is from another place."

The Kingdom of God will remain not of this world until the Lord returns at the time given by the Father resulting in the battle of Armageddon. So, if the pope has a power and authority to dominate the kings and nations of the world, then it is not from God. It is instead from the power of Babylon who was granted by God for its kingdom to be, "of this world."

NIV Jn 18:37 "You are a king, then!" said Pilate. Jesus answered, "You are right in saying I am a king. In fact, for this reason I was born, and for this I came into the world, to testify to the truth. Everyone on the side of truth listens to me."

NIV Jn 19:8 When Pilate heard this, he was even more afraid,
NIV Jn 19:9 and he went back inside the palace. "Where do you come from?" he asked Jesus, but Jesus gave him no answer.
NIV Jn 19:10 "Do you refuse to speak to me?" Pilate said. "Don't you realize I have power either to free you or to crucify you?"
NIV Jn 19:11 Jesus answered, "You would have no power over me if it were not given to you from above.

Until it is His time to return, the Father has given the power and authority of the earth over to the beast.

No, it is not by the Holy Spirit. The popery starting with Leo III have been classic Jezebel. The pope is not the king of the Holy Roman Empire, but she sits as a queen. The pope is not the king of the Holy Roman Empire, but through intrigue, lies, and deceit she rules from behind the scenes. The pope is not the king of the Holy Roman Empire who controls the people, but whispers in his ear and controls the king. Is it any wonder that Jesus called her (the Church), "Jezebel" and said of her in the fourth Church Age of Thyatira:

NIV Rev 2:18b These are the words of the Son of God, whose eyes are like blazing fire and whose feet are like burnished bronze.
NIV Rev 2:19 I know your deeds, your love and faith, your service and perseverance, and that you are now doing more than you did at first.
NIV Rev 2:20 Nevertheless, I have this against you: You tolerate that woman Jezebel, who calls herself a prophetess. By her teaching she misleads my servants into sexual immorality and the eating of food sacrificed to idols.
NIV Rev 2:21 I have given her time to repent of her immorality, but she is unwilling.
NIV Rev 2:22 So I will cast her on a bed of suffering, and I will make those who commit adultery with her suffer intensely, unless they repent of her ways.
NIV Rev 2:23 I will strike her children dead. Then all the churches will know that I am he who searches hearts and minds, and I will repay each of you according to your deeds.

The kings and nations who committed adultery with her suffered greatly through almost constant war, including the Thirty Years War and the One Hundred Years War, to name only two. Germany was devastated as a nation as a result. It says the Lord holds against the people, His people, that they tolerate her vain power over the nations. He decreed that as a consequence He would put her on a bed of suffering, striking her children dead. This was fulfilled when the black plague swept over Christian Europe killing more than half of Europe's population. Yet, we still do not see the pope and the Roman Catholic Church as the seventh head of the beast and the kingdom of Babylon.

NIV Rev 18:4 *Then I heard another voice from heaven say:*

"Come out of her, my people,

so that you will not share in her sins,

so that you will not receive any of her plagues;
NIV Rev 18:5 *for her sins are piled up to heaven,*
and God has remembered her crimes.

This narrative again is recounting the warnings and testimony of the two witnesses at this part of the story:

NRSV Rev 14:9 *Then another angel, a third, followed them* (the second of the two witnesses), *crying with a loud voice, "Those who worship the beast and its image, and receive a mark on their foreheads or on their hands, ¹⁰ they will also drink the wine of God's wrath, poured unmixed into the cup of his anger, and they will be tormented with fire and sulfur in the presence of the holy angels and in the presence of the Lamb. ¹¹ And the smoke of their torment goes up forever and ever. There is no rest day or night for those who worship the beast and its image and for anyone who receives the mark of its name."*

It is here we can realize that when they come, the two witnesses will rail against the Roman Catholic Church as a part of their testimony. Disowning her, condemning her for her sins, and calling her Babylon, they cry out to the world. They continue saying that God will destroy her, while calling for the people to abandon her. Is there any wonder that the pope/false prophet searches for a way to shut them up? They will expose to the whole world all the sins, and crimes against both God and their fellow man. The two witnesses will reject the *Church Corrupt* and its leadership more severely than John the Baptist did when he said to the Pharisees and Sadducees:

NLT Mt 3:5 *People from Jerusalem and from every section of Judea and from all over the Jordan Valley went out to the wilderness to hear him preach.*
NLT Mt 3:6 *And when they confessed their sins, he baptized them in the Jordan River.*
NLT Mt 3:7 *But when he saw many Pharisees and Sadducees coming to be baptized, he denounced them. "You brood of snakes!" he exclaimed. "Who warned you to flee God's coming judgment?*
NLT Mt 3:8 *Prove by the way you live that you have really turned from your sins and turned to God.*
NLT Mt 3:9 *Don't just say, 'We're safe—we're the descendants of Abraham.' That proves nothing. God can change these stones here into children of Abraham.*

John is not just talking to and about the Pharisees and Sadducees but is prophesying about the very end, even the time of the rapture and the great tribulation. It is said of the Roman Catholic Church whose pope is the false prophet will also say to herself in a similar way as the Pharisees and Sadducees said to themselves:

> *NIV Rev 18:6 Give back to her as she has given;*
> *pay her back double for what she has done.*
> *Mix her a double portion from her own cup.*
> *NIV Rev 18:7 Give her as much torture and grief*
> *as the glory and luxury she gave herself.*
> *In her heart she boasts,*
> *'I sit as queen; I am not a widow,*
> *and I will never mourn.'*

She thinks she is the bride and queen of Christ, the King of kings, and Lord of lords. Since He lives forever, she thinks she is not a widow and will never mourn. However, in the seventh letter to the Church, the Lord says He spits her out of His mouth—divorces her because of her adulteries. Verses 6 and 7 also say something much different, making her in denial of her true circumstances and standing. It is just as John continues to prophesy about the end:

NLT Mt 3:10 Even now the ax of God's judgment is poised, ready to sever your roots. Yes, every tree that does not produce good fruit will be chopped down and thrown into the fire.
NLT Mt 3:11 "I baptize with water those who turn from their sins and turn to God. But someone is coming soon who is far greater than I am—so much greater that I am not even worthy to be his slave. He will baptize you with the Holy Spirit and with fire.
NLT Mt 3:12 He is ready to separate the chaff from the grain (wheat) with his winnowing fork. Then he will clean up the threshing area, storing the grain in his barn but burning the chaff with never-ending fire."

The separating of the chaff from the wheat is the same as separating the wheat from the darnel in a parable of Jesus'. It divides those in His Church from the ones the Lord takes up in the rapture, from those who must endure the fires of the great tribulation.

How is the testimony of the two witnesses pertinent to the punishment of the woman who rides the beast? It is pertinent because of what the pope does after being totally exposed and stripped naked having his and the Roman Catholic Church's sins exposed to the whole world. It is a moment in the valley of decision that the two witnesses will force them to show their true colors, the pope/false prophet and the Roman Catholic Church! All the extreme things which were spoken and written about them, including all the articles on the internet which rail against them (which nobody can scarcely believe), will at this moment be proven true or false.

It has already begun to happen that the pope of the Roman Catholic Church is attempting to regain the glory and authority over the whole world the Roman Church once had. The current Pope Francis is busy on a mission to reconcile and unite all the different Christian religions, as well as all the world religions. Likewise, he is attempting to bring unity and peace between the nations. Just as he helped negotiate a treaty between the USA and Cuba, he will begin to make a treaty with many nations making himself and the Catholic Church the great mediator, but the secret motives will be to hold all the strings.

In addition, these treaties do not stop with making treaties with nations, the pope will make treaties with other Christian denominations and with other religions in the name of unity and peace for mankind. Indeed, this too has already begun to happen. Pope Francis has signed treaties between their once rivals the Lutherans and the Protestants healing the chasm between them and creating relationships with eastern religions. However, it is an acceptance without conformity because the Catholic Church has not changed her ways.

In the end, the world and naive Christians will find out too late! The popery is doing this so that he may present to the beast this huge contingency of followers from around the globe for the beast to rule over. He is preparing the way for the returned beast. To give the beast all the Christians as his subject is the greatest "bait and switch" deception ever perpetrated on the entire globe in all of its history.

Cloaked behind a pretense of peace, dishing out acceptance without conformity to everyone in the name of brotherhood and unity. All in an effort to position the popery above all the nations and world religions as Pope Leo III did before him. Just as the false prophet positions himself exactly where he wants to be, the two witnesses will expose the motives, sins, and crimes of the popery for what it really is. The two witnesses will expose the sins of the world as well.

NLT Rev 13:11 *Then I saw another beast come up out of the earth. He had two horns like those of a lamb, and he spoke with the voice of a dragon.*
NLT Rev 13:12 *He exercised all the authority of the first beast. And he required all the earth and those who belong to this world to worship the first beast, whose death-wound had been healed.*

Will the pope and the Catholic Church confess their sins, repent, and give up their power over the world? For in the valley of decision there are only two ways: give up all that they have become or fight to hang on to it. The one who was worthy to open the scroll, having exclusive knowledge of the plan for judgment and redemption and is the sole spirit of prophecy tells us beforehand: that the pope/false prophet will want to hang onto his power over the world, then denounce the two witnesses as not from God, but blasphemers.

In a rage, the pope will rally the whole world together as one voice, one heart, and one mind to kill the two witnesses at any cost, to shut them up and stop their plagues. He will not stand by and let the two witnesses destroy the power base he worked so hard to build, by exposing his real agenda. In large part, it is the message of the two witnesses that exposes the Roman Catholic Church and the pope for who they are and what their standing with God truly is.

The pope/false prophet will seal his fate by entering the temple he had stopped the sacrifices in 3-1/2 years previously. He will call the disembodied Nimrod back from among the dead in the Abyss. The pope will clothe the disembodied (dead) Nimrod with that image he created so that he has a body to come back to life with. Then the beast, the risen Nimrod, will leave the temple and kill the unkillable, the two witnesses.

The two witnesses will only die because their mission is complete. By the pope's actions against them, the two witnesses have, by giving up their lives, exposed the true heart and motives of the pope as the false prophet. They prove him as hateful and in rebellion to God. Why? So that the saints inside the Church will see the Roman Catholic Church is beyond a doubt, not of God. They prove with their very lives that the pope is the false prophet, and in turn the Christians wake up from their delusion. Then, they "come out of her" no longer remaining hell-bound for the lake of fire. Instead they become the great multitude who are raised as celestial humans during the first resurrection.

Although they will wake from their delusion too late, hundreds of millions even numbers over a billion will rather be killed than to follow the false prophet and the beast once they are revealed for who they really are, and who they really serve. They will do as the two witnesses told them and be saved as God's own.

Paul tells us about this in 2 Thessalonians. He explains that Jesus cannot return until this deed by the pope is done:

NRSV 2Th 2:1 As to the coming of our Lord Jesus Christ and our being gathered together to him, we beg you, brothers and sisters, 2 not to be quickly shaken in mind or alarmed, either by spirit or by word or by letter, as though from us, to the effect that the day of the Lord is already here. 3 Let no one deceive you in any way; for that day will not come unless (the apostasy) the rebellion comes first and the lawless one is revealed, the one destined for destruction. 4 He opposes and exalts himself above every so-called god or object of worship, so that he takes his seat in the temple of God, declaring himself to be God.

Verses 3 and 4 (above) are talking about the work of two different figures. They are, the beast out of the sea, and the beast out of the earth. They are better known as the antichrist/beast and the false prophet/pope. The rebellion and apostasy which must come first is what facilitates the "revealing" of the lawless one. Let us take a look at that same verse 3 in the amplified version to get a more detailed description:

Amp 2Th 2:3 Let no one deceive or beguile you in any way, for that day will not come except the apostasy comes first [unless the predicted great 2 falling away of those who have professed to be Christians has come], and the man of lawlessness (sin) is revealed, who is the son of doom (of perdition),
Amp 2Th 2:4 Who opposes and exalts himself so proudly and insolently against and over all that is called God or that is worshiped, [even to his actually] taking his seat in the temple of God, proclaiming that he himself is God.

Here is the definition of the word apostasy: the abandonment or renunciation of a religious or political belief.

It should be asked, what is this renunciation and rebellion (the falling away of Christians) which must come first, all about? During their day the apostles taught that there was going to be a rebellion by the Christians against God; a renunciation of their faith by those who are not in union with the Lord, but are, by profession only, Christians. This is the reaction that the *Church Corrupt,* and superficial Christians who are so by profession only will have against the two witnesses. They will hate them, denouncing them as not from God or representing the Church.

The reason is because the two witnesses will expose the hypocrisies in the Church, while emphasizing their points with bringing down plagues around the globe just as Moses did in Egypt, on a local scale. They will want them killed. When nobody can succeed, the pope will enter the temple 30 days after the last seven of the 70-7's promised to the Jews has ended. In the temple he will create an image of the beast, calling him back from the dead to occupy that image and therefore come alive. He will then force everyone to worship the beast and take his mark under penalty of death. The beast/antichrist will set up his throne in the temple and exalt himself above every god there is and every object that is worshiped, even the Creator and Christian God. It is then that Jerusalem becomes the great city who rules over the nations of the earth (Babylon).

Amp 2Th 2:5 Do you not remember that I told you these things when I was still with you? 6 And you know what is now restraining him, so that he may be revealed when his time comes. 7 For the mystery of lawlessness is already at work, but only until the one who now restrains it is removed.

The mystery of lawlessness is already at work since the rebellion of Nimrod and his seven heads. The Pope and his Roman Catholic Church is the seventh and final head before Nimrod returns on his way to his destruction.

The pope orchestrates the rebellion, then denounces the two witnesses and the Lord, forcing everyone to worship the risen beast. The rebellion and denouncing of the two witnesses are followed by the revealing of the source of lawlessness—the beast/antichrist raised back to life. After the two witnesses are killed, they raise from the dead 3-1/2 days later. Then, along with the Holy Spirit and those in union with Christ, they abandon the earth leaving it to its own evil in a global desolation. The great tribulation begins. 3-1/2 years later the great tribulation ends with the sign of the Son of Man in the sky, and the beginning of the punishment of Babylon in the world. 3-1/2 years after that, the first resurrection and second rapture occur with its recipients who rise to meet Jesus in the sky. It is then, after all that, Jesus will touch down on the Mount of Olives bringing back with Him the New Jerusalem and His entourage of angels and celestial humans.

Amp 2Th 2:8 And then the lawless one will be revealed (come to life in the temple in Jerusalem), *whom the Lord Jesus will destroy with the breath of his mouth, annihilating him by the manifestation of his coming. 9 The coming of the lawless one is apparent in the working of Satan, who uses all power, signs, lying wonders, 10 and every kind of wicked deception for those who are perishing, because they refused to love the truth and so be saved. 11 For this reason God sends them a powerful delusion, leading them to believe what is false, 12 so that all who have not believed the truth but took pleasure in unrighteousness will be condemned.*

When the Corrupt Christians and world hate the two witnesses it is because they refuse to love the truth as Jesus told us judgment is based on:

Amp Jn 3:19 The [basis of the] judgment (indictment, the test by which men are judged, the ground for the sentence) lies in this: the Light has come into the world, and people have loved the darkness rather than and more than the Light, for their works (deeds) were evil.
Amp Jn 3:20 For every wrongdoer hates (loathes, detests) the Light, and will not come out into the Light but shrinks from it, lest his works (his deeds, his activities, his conduct) be exposed and reproved.
Amp Jn 3:21 But he who practices truth [who does what is right] comes out into the Light; so that his works may be plainly shown to be what they are—wrought with God [divinely prompted, done with God's help, in dependence upon Him].

NIV Rev 18:8 Therefore in one day her plagues will overtake her:

death, mourning and famine.

She will be consumed by fire,

for mighty is the Lord God who judges her.

Note: When it says, ". . . mighty is the Lord God who judges her," it is clearing up a big point of contention. The great tribulation is the Lord punishing and redeeming the *Church Corrupt.*

It will indeed be a suddenly from God that in a day all life in the world will change. On the same day that the two witnesses rise up into the sky, those in union with Christ will likewise be lifted up to heaven. The Holy Spirit will withdraw from the earth leaving it in a global desolation—an absence of the presence of God. An earthquake will destroy a tenth of Jerusalem and seven thousand people will die (Rev 11:13). The pope/false prophet will make everyone around the world worship the beast or be killed. The Church will lose all station, and stature in the world. They will lose all their wealth, power, and property.

It says above she will be consumed with fire. Fire consumes everything it burns, leaving no part left except for the ashes on the ground and the smoke that rises up into the sky. Everything, no matter what it is, turns into the same thing, ashes, when it is consumed with fire. Its former state is unrecognizable and becomes the same as everything else consumed with fire, ashes and smoke. The judgment of God is that the *Church Corrupt* will be totally consumed as with a fire of punishments, which leaves no trace or evidence of it having existed, but only a heap of ashes (of its destruction) and smoke rising up to heaven. Finally, after those measures, the *Church Corrupt* is torn away from Babylon by its rejection and hatred of the Church. She has become free to return to her first love just as Gomer was freed from her lovers by their rejection of her.

> WEB Rev 18:9 *The kings of the earth, who committed sexual immorality and lived wantonly with her, will weep and wail over her, when they look at the smoke of her burning, [10] standing far away for the fear of her torment, saying, 'Woe, woe, the great city, Babylon, the strong city! For your judgment has come in one hour.' [11] The merchants of the earth weep and mourn over her, for no one buys their merchandise any more; [12] merchandise of gold, silver, precious stones, pearls, fine linen, purple, silk, scarlet, all expensive wood, every vessel of ivory, every vessel made of most precious wood, and of brass, and iron, and marble; [13] and cinnamon, incense, perfume, frankincense, wine, olive oil, fine flour, wheat, sheep, horses, chariots, and people's bodies and souls. [14] The fruits which your soul lusted after have been lost to you, and all things that were dainty and sumptuous have perished from you, and you will find them no more at all. [15] The merchants of these things, who were made rich by her, will stand far away for the fear of her torment, weeping and mourning; [16a] saying, 'Woe, woe, the great city, she who was dressed in fine linen, <u>purple, and scarlet</u>,*

At the end of this discourse describing the fearful and sudden dismantling of Babylon it says, "the great city who was dressed in fine linen, purple and scarlet." This tells us something very important; it verifies what it says in the opening of this narrative, that John is being shown the punishment of the great prostitute. In addition, it reveals that the great prostitute is the Roman Catholic Church whose head is seated in Rome, and whose colors are purple and scarlet. The entire *Church Corrupt* who was left behind and opposed the two witnesses are consumed by fire with her.

By these verses above (18:9-16) we also know that when it says this is the punishment of Babylon, that it is Babylon in the Church only. For the kings and nations, the power brokers and the merchants are in a fearful awe, even stunned as they look on at the destruction and killing of the *Church Corrupt*. Just as the towns people of Nazi Germany stood by, stunned as the Jews were collected, brought to concentration camps, ending in mass genocide.

However, the kings and nations, the power brokers and the merchants are Babylon in the world, ruled by the ten horns, the false prophet, and the beast/antichrist. They are at this point onlookers. It is not yet their time. All these things are so far the punishment of the *Church Corrupt* or Babylon in the Church! Although their time is coming and will fall upon them even more suddenly, with more and harder crushing blows, this narrative continues below with describing the punishment of the *Church Corrupt*.

> WEB Rev 18:16b ... *and decked with gold and precious stones and pearls!* [17] *For in an hour such great riches are made desolate.' Every ship master, and everyone who sails anywhere, and mariners, and as many as gain their living by sea, stood far away,* [18] *and cried out as they looked at the smoke of her burning, saying, 'What is like the great city?'* [19] *They cast dust on their heads, and cried, weeping and mourning, saying, 'Woe, woe, the great city, in which all who had their ships in the sea were made rich by reason of her great wealth!' For she is made desolate in one hour.*

In the above verses the world mourns both out of fear and for selfish reasons. They are also astonished how something that great and established can be brought down so suddenly. However, (below) all of heaven is called to rejoice over the utter destruction of the Roman Catholic Church and the balance of the *Church Corrupt*.

> WEB Rev 18:20 *"Rejoice over her, O heaven, you saints, apostles, and prophets; for God has judged your judgment on her."* [21] *A mighty angel took up a stone like a great millstone and cast it into the sea, saying, "Thus with violence will Babylon, the great city, be thrown down, and will be found no more at all.* [22] *The voice of harpists, minstrels, flute players, and trumpeters will be heard no more at all in you. No craftsman, of whatever craft, will be found any more at all in you. The sound of a mill will be heard no more at all in you.* [23a] <u>*The light of a lamp will shine no more at all in you. The voice of the bridegroom and of the bride will be heard no more at all in you;*</u>

The destruction of the Church is so thorough, that it says the voice of the bridegroom (the Lord) and of the bride (His Church) will be heard no more at all in her (the Church). We will learn later that it is Israel and their form of worship that will continue during the 1,000 year reign of Christ, and not the practices of the Church. However, from the Church will come the majority of all the celestial humans who will rule with the Lord as ministers of His Kingdom.

WEB Rev 18:23b for your merchants were the princes of the earth; for with your sorcery all the nations were deceived. ²⁴ In her was found the blood of prophets and of saints, and of all who have been slain on the earth."

Verse 23b (above) tells us the charges against her. In her bid for power, she has lied, seduced, and hypnotized the world, even her own (the Christians) by boasting and blinding them with a spirit of delusion. In order to hang onto her power, she has betrayed, tortured and slaughtered her own in numbers at least ten times greater than the Roman Empire. We may have forgotten her crimes, even become oblivious to their relevance. The dead have not, as we see below, nor has the Lord.

WEB Rev 19:1 After these things I heard something like a loud voice of a great multitude in heaven, saying, "Hallelujah! Salvation, power, and glory belong to our God: ² for true and righteous are his judgments. For he has judged the great prostitute, who corrupted the earth with her sexual immorality, and he has avenged the blood of his servants at her hand." ³ A second said, "Hallelujah! Her smoke goes up forever and ever." ⁴ The twenty-four elders and the four living creatures fell down and worshiped God who sits on the throne, saying, "Amen! Hallelujah!" ⁵ A voice came from the throne, saying, "Give praise to our God, all you his servants, you who fear him, the small and the great!" ⁶ I heard something like the voice of a great multitude, and like the voice of many waters, and like the voice of mighty thunders, saying, "Hallelujah! For the Lord our God, the Almighty, reigns! ⁷ᵃ Let us rejoice and be exceedingly glad, and let us give the glory to him.

Starting with verse 19:1 (above) we have come to the end of the destruction of Babylon in the Church. No longer are the merchants, the kings, and the nations standing by watching as the *Church Corrupt* gets Babylon torn out of her. Babylon has rejected her, and she has denounced Babylon while instead holding fast to her first love. The tables have turned, and it is them, Babylon in the world, who is now being thoroughly destroyed. The great multitude, having together a voice as one which is thunderous, even deafening like the sound of a waterfall, are those who endured the great tribulation while standing fast to their testimony. They are now together in their full numbers which signifies that the great tribulation has been brought to a screeching halt.

NIV Rev 7:9 After this I looked and there before me was a great multitude that no one could count, from every nation, tribe, people and language, standing before the throne and in front of the Lamb. They were wearing white robes and were holding palm branches in their hands.
NIV Rev 7:10 And they cried out in a loud voice: "Salvation belongs to our God, who sits on the throne, and to the Lamb."
NIV Rev 7:11 All the angels were standing around the throne and around the elders and the four living creatures. They fell down on their faces before the throne and worshiped God,

NIV Rev 7:12 saying: "Amen! Praise and glory and wisdom and thanks and honor and power and strength be to our God for ever and ever. Amen!"

NIV Rev 7:13 Then one of the elders asked me, "These in white robes—who are they, and where did they come from?"

NIV Rev 7:14 I answered, "Sir, you know." And he said, "These are they who have come out of the great tribulation; they have washed their robes and made them white in the blood of the Lamb.

NIV Rev 7:15 Therefore, "they are before the throne of God and serve him day and night in his temple; and he who sits on the throne will spread his tent over them.

NIV Rev 7:16 Never again will they hunger; never again will they thirst. The sun will not beat upon them, nor any scorching heat.

NIV Rev 7:17 For the Lamb at the center of the throne will be their shepherd; he will lead them to springs of living water. And God will wipe away every tear from their eyes."

As a result, and in a day, all life on earth has changed turning against the beast and his kingdom. That is not spoken of here because this part has always been about informing John of the punishment of the prostitute who rides the beast. Nevertheless, it is at this time when the 1/2 hour of silence or inactivity in heaven is over. Heaven will punish the world. Four trumpet blasts and bowls are poured out on the earth's inhabitants. In addition, one of the three woes have been released on the earth simultaneously, making life on earth pure hell. The fact that this is the end of the great tribulation is supported further by the verse below. The marriage of the Lamb has come and His wife has made herself ready by being purified through the great tribulation! Not another Christian who hangs fast to his testimony in Christ will ever be killed again!

> *WEB Rev 19:7b* For the marriage of the Lamb has come, and his wife has made herself ready." *8* It was given to her that she would array herself in bright, pure, fine linen: for the fine linen is the righteous acts of the saints. *9* He said to me, "Write, 'Blessed are those who are invited to the marriage supper of the Lamb.'" He said to me, "These are true words of God." *10* I fell down before his feet to worship him. He said to me, "Look! Don't do it! I am a fellow bondservant with you and with your brothers who hold the testimony of Jesus. Worship God, for the testimony of Jesus is the Spirit of Prophecy."

"These are the true words of God." How incredibly vivid these visions must have been. How consuming and a part of them they made John to be. This is not something you would soon forget. It says about John in the beginning:

Amp Rev 5:3 And no one in heaven or on earth or under the earth [in the realm of the dead, Hades] was able to open the scroll or to take a [single] look at its contents.

Amp Rev 5:4 And I wept audibly and bitterly because no one was found fit to open the scroll or to inspect it.

He wept from the depths of his soul, audibly and bitterly when no one was found worthy to simply open and see the contents of the scroll. He did so even before he knew what it contained or its importance. This scene he became part of was so much bigger and beyond himself it was overwhelming. Then John gets to see the harsh reality of what happens to the Church he loves so much and would gladly die for. He sees what she is to become, the great prostitute who becomes one of the seven heads of the beast. How could that be, but there it was right before his eyes.

Amp Rev 17:4 The woman was robed in purple and scarlet and bedecked with gold, precious stones, and pearls, [and she was] holding in her hand a golden cup full of the accursed offenses and the filth of her lewdness and vice.

Amp Rev 17:5 And on her forehead there was inscribed a name of mystery [with a secret symbolic meaning]: Babylon the great, the mother of prostitutes (idolatresses) and of the filth and atrocities and abominations of the earth.

Amp Rev 17:6 I also saw that the woman was drunk, [drunk] with the blood of the saints (God's people) and the blood of the martyrs [who witnessed] for Jesus. And when I saw her, I was utterly amazed and wondered greatly.

Amp Rev 17:7 But the angel said to me, Why do you wonder? I will explain to you the [secret symbolic meaning of the] mystery of the woman, as well as of the beast having the seven heads and ten horns that carries her.

NRSV Rev 17:1 Then one of the seven angels who had the seven bowls came and said to me, "Come, I will show you the judgment of the great whore who is seated on many waters, ² with whom the kings of the earth have committed fornication, and with the wine of whose fornication the inhabitants of the earth have become drunk." ³ So he carried me away in the spirit into a wilderness, and I saw a woman sitting on a scarlet beast that was full of blasphemous names, and it had seven heads and ten horns. ⁴ The woman was clothed in purple and scarlet, and adorned with gold and jewels and pearls, holding in her hand a golden cup full of abominations and the impurities of her fornication; ⁵ and on her forehead was written a name, a mystery: "Babylon the great, mother of whores and of earth's abominations." ⁶ And I saw that the woman was drunk with the blood of the saints and the blood of the witnesses to Jesus.

When I saw her, I was greatly amazed (and wondered) *⁷ But the angel said to me, "Why are you so amazed* (and wonder)?
I will tell you the mystery of the woman, and of the beast with seven heads and ten horns that carries her.

John is told by the angel that he will be told the mystery of the woman. He was astonished, overwhelmed, even dumfounded looking at this woman. He scarcely believed what he saw, but he knew who the woman was. The question is, how did she turn into that? That is the mystery! I will tell you the mystery of how the woman became what she is pictured as, and also, I will tell you of her punishment, he is told. If John became so much a part of these visions and their realities were so vivid that he wept until his guts turned inside out at the news of the scroll, how much more will he be astonished at what the Church turns into? How could he keep himself composed? The Church is everything he has given his life for.

Then he sees the final end of it. He sees how, through her punishment, Babylon is torn away from her, and they become the great multitude in heaven with celestial bodies. There is hope! The Lord finishes the work that He began in them! The Lord is greater and more merciful than their sins, John witnesses this in his vision. Is there any wonder that he falls at the feet of this angel who shared the outcome? Just the sheer emotional weight of what he was shown is one thing. Then considering that he finally reached the end of the intensity of this story, and followed by the outcome must have overwhelmed him, even unglued him. Praise God we have record, and both know the truth and outcome of it all. The contents of the scroll is the testimony of Jesus, and He is the Spirit of prophecy.

Notes

² Zoller, J. *Pope Gregory VII and King Henry IV*. Retrieved June 2018, from Mr. Zoller's Blog:
https://misterzoller.files.wordpress.com/2014/04/popesvskings_henrygregory.pdf

---

CHAPTER 3

The Rider on the White Horse

The Sign of the Lord's Coming

WEB Rev 19:11 <u>I saw the heaven (standing) opened</u>, *and behold, a white horse, and he who sat on it is called Faithful and True. In righteousness he judges and makes war.*

The last vision brought us to the end of the great tribulation. This vision which follows is the sign of the Son of Man poised to return to the earth.

NRSV Rev 6:12 *When he opened the sixth seal, I looked, and there came a great earthquake; the sun became black as sackcloth, the full moon became like blood, *[13]* and the stars of the sky fell to the earth as the fig tree drops its winter fruit when shaken by a gale.*

The above verse 12 describes the global desolation of God's presence being withdrawn from the earth because of the abomination performed by the false prophet of bringing Nimrod back from the dead. It starts with a huge earthquake, and the rapture of the Christians who are in union with the Holy Spirit. "Black as sackcloth" is a metaphor for the spiritual darkness on the earth resulting in God's Spirit having left. The great tribulation ensues and the Christians who are left behind, the *Church Corrupt*, die in groves like the stars of heaven falling to the ground, or figs being blown off their trees. The moment the tribulation is over and the full number of those who would be killed, die, God brings His influence and wrath back to the earth. That begins below, in verse 14, with the sign of the coming of the Son of Man.

NRSV Rev 6:14 *The sky vanished like a scroll rolling itself up, and every mountain and island was removed from its place. ¹⁵ Then the kings of the earth and the magnates* (the rich and power brokers) *and the generals and the rich and the powerful, and everyone, slave and free, hid in the caves and among the rocks of the mountains, ¹⁶ calling to the mountains and rocks, "Fall on us <u>and hide us from the face of the one seated on the throne and from the wrath of the Lamb;</u> ¹⁷ <u>for the great day of their wrath has come, and who is able to stand?"</u>*

Again below, Jesus is asked by His Apostles, "what will be the sign of Your coming?" and Jesus replied by speaking the following verses. He starts with the withdrawal of His Spirit from the earth because of the global desolation caused by the false prophet and the arrival of the beast coming back to life from out of the Abyss.

NRSV Mt 24:15 *"So when you see the desolating sacrilege* (the beast back from the dead) *standing in the holy place, as was spoken of by the prophet Daniel (let the reader understand), ¹⁶ then those in Judea must flee to the mountains; ¹⁷ the one on the housetop must not go down to take what is in the house; ¹⁸ the one in the field must not turn back to get a coat. ¹⁹ Woe to those who are pregnant and to those who are nursing infants in those days! ²⁰ Pray that your flight may not be in winter or on a sabbath. ²¹ For at that time there will be great suffering, such as has not been from the beginning of the world until now, no, and never will be* (the great tribulation when hundreds of millions die for their faith). *²² And if those days had not been cut short, no one would be saved; but for the sake of the elect those days will be cut short. ²³ Then if anyone says to you, 'Look! Here is the Messiah! or 'There he is!--do not believe it. ²⁴ For false messiahs and false prophets will appear and produce great signs and omens, to lead astray, if possible, even the elect. ²⁵ Take note, I have told you beforehand. ²⁶ So, if they say to you, 'Look! He is in the wilderness,' do not go out. If they say, 'Look! He is in the inner rooms,' do not believe it. ²⁷ <u>For as the lightning comes from the east and flashes as far as the west, so will be the coming of the Son of Man.</u> ²⁸ Wherever the corpse is, there the vultures will gather.*

"Wherever the corpse is, there the vultures will gather." By saying this proverb Jesus is reminding us that when there is disaster and the people become desperate for hope and relief, all the liars, cheaters, thieves, imposters, and carpet baggers come out of the woodwork like cockroaches. He tells them do not even bother to check out all the rumors or any claim that He has returned. Jesus is reminding them that the earth will be under a total global desolation for 3-1/2 years! God has agreed to give His authority of the earth and its inhabitants over to the beast and false prophet, until His plan is carried out. People are deceived if they believe a single prayer will be answered during this time period. He is telling them, when I come back, you will know. It will be a spectacle in the sky and will be seen from horizon to horizon. That will be the sign of My coming! It is also why if there are rumors about Me being back, you don't even have to bother checking them out to know that they are false.

Amp Rev 17:16 And the ten horns that you saw, they and the beast will [be the very ones to] hate the harlot (the idolatrous woman); they will make her cheerless (bereaved, desolate), and they will strip her and eat up her flesh and utterly consume her with fire.
Amp Rev 17:17 For God has put it into their hearts to carry out His own purpose by acting in harmony in surrendering their royal power and authority to the beast, until the prophetic words (intentions and promises) of God shall be fulfilled.

NIV Rev 13:9 He who has an ear, let him hear.
NIV Rev 13:10 If anyone is to go into captivity, into captivity he will go. If anyone is to be killed with the sword, with the sword he will be killed.
This calls for patient endurance and faithfulness on the part of the saints.

Jesus started out this discourse in answer to His Apostles asking what will be the sign of His coming. Jesus finally tells them here, do not bother checking out any claims, they all will be false because the earth is in a global desolation. However, when I come, you will know beyond a shadow of a doubt it is Me because of the sign of My return: "as the lightning comes from the east and flashes as far as the west, so will be the coming of the Son of Man." He is saying the sign will be in the sky and the whole earth will see it from horizon to horizon.

Now (below) Jesus tells us the exact timing. He is saying that the exact moment the great tribulation is complete, the sign of the Son of Man will come.

NRSV Mt 24:29 "Immediately after the suffering of those days the sun will be darkened, and the moon will not give its light; the stars will fall from heaven, and the powers of heaven will be shaken. 30 Then (immediately after that) the sign of the Son of Man will appear in heaven, and then all the tribes of the earth will mourn, and they will see 'the Son of Man coming on the clouds of heaven' with power and great glory.

It is exactly as spoken of in the sixth seal. Those on the earth will mourn at this sight in the sky, realizing their time is finished.

NRSV Mt 24:31 *And he will send out his angels with a loud trumpet call, and they will gather his elect from the four winds, from one end of heaven to the other.*

As Jesus remains in the sky poised to come down and take over the earth, the first resurrection of the dead will happen. Those who were not killed will join those resurrected and be caught up in the sky, lining up behind Jesus ready to return with Him. Only they now have become celestial humans.

> *Rev 19:12* *His eyes are a flame of fire, and on his head are many crowns. He has names written and a name written which no one knows but he himself.* *13* *He is clothed in a garment sprinkled with blood. His name is called "The Word of God."* *14* *The armies which are in heaven followed him on white horses, clothed in white, pure, fine linen.*

This moment is so significant! In the Garden, God said that the child of Eve will crush the head of the serpent. Through the prophets, the Lord spoke that He will crush the Assyrian (Nimrod, the antichrist, and beast) on His holy mountain.

NIV Isa 14:25a *I will crush the Assyrian in my land; on my mountains I will trample him down.*

Now is finally the time! For the great city that rules the kings of the earth (Babylon) is no longer Rome, but Jerusalem where the beast is to be raised from the dead!

Back in history, the greatest army ever assembled up to that time was the Assyrian Army. They came and destroyed or took into captivity all of the 10 tribes of Israel and Judah except the city of Jerusalem, the capitol of Judah. Then, that great army of overwhelming numbers surrounded Jerusalem beginning their siege of it. It was the undoing of God's people behind the walls. However, it was not the designated time ordained by God, and the Assyrian/Nimrod was not alive, nor was his empire a global one yet. As a result, the Lord sent an angel and when they had awoken to continue their siege 185,000 of the Assyrians lay dead, causing them to withdraw back to Assyria—even flee leaving all their provisions for this great army and the booty they had captured.

God had revealed His plan to His prophet Micah. Saying that He will not allow Babylon to attain global domination until the time of His choosing and according to His purposes. In order to impede Babylon's destiny of global domination until the right time, God gave the beast 7 heads, or seven shepherds (kings). Each of the seven kings would take over the previous, only after destroying the former with war. In this way Babylon takes centuries in order to finally reach its destiny.

NIV Mic 5:5b . . . *When the Assyrian invades our land and marches through our fortresses, we will raise against him seven shepherds, even eight leaders of men.*
NIV Mic 5:6 *They will rule the land of Assyria with the sword, the land of Nimrod with drawn sword. He* (the Christ) *will deliver us from the Assyrian when he invades our land and marches into our borders*

The reason all this is significant is because now the time is right according to the purposes of God. Nimrod, AKA the Assyrian, is risen, and is on God's holy mountain. Jerusalem is now the great city, Babylon, who rules ALL the kings of the earth. The stage is set. In the past, the great and numerous Assyrian Army had laid siege to Jerusalem, terrifying its inhabitants, making sure they had no escape, while stealing away all hope of survival. Now, in the sky from horizon to horizon the Lord lay siege not against a city as they did, but against the entire earth which is the kingdom of the beast.

The inhabitants of the earth are terrified at the sight of Jesus in the sky with His army surrounding the earth. There is no place to escape. The Assyrians would mound up earth against every door out of the city, trapping them inside. Then starve its inhabitants weakening both their morale and physical strength before the assault. The Lord surrounds the earth while pummeling it with acts of God, natural disasters, and woes administered by supernatural beings before invading the earth. Again, it says of this sight and of all the disasters and woes:

NRSV Rev 6:14 *The sky vanished like a scroll rolling itself up, and every mountain and island was removed from its place.* [15] *Then the kings of the earth and the magnates and the generals and the rich and the powerful, and everyone, slave and free, hid in the caves and among the rocks of the mountains,* [16] *calling to the mountains and rocks, "Fall on us and hide us from the face of the one seated on the throne and from the wrath of the Lamb;* [17] *for the great day of their wrath has come, and who is able to stand?"*

Now this vision of the rider on the white horse, brings us beyond His return and below tells us of the third woe, which is the battle of Armageddon. With this battle, as described below, Jesus takes over Lordship of the entire globe, and utterly destroys the kingdom of the beast.

> *NIV Rev 19:15 Out of his mouth comes a <u>sharp sword</u> with which to strike down the nations. "He will rule them with an iron scepter." He treads the winepress of the fury of the wrath of God Almighty.*

> *WEB Rev 19:16 He has on his garment and on his thigh a name written,*

> *"KING OF KINGS, AND LORD OF LORDS."*

> *17 I saw an angel standing in the sun. He cried with a loud voice, saying to all the birds that fly in the sky, "Come! Be gathered together to the great supper of God, 18 that you may eat the flesh of kings, the flesh of captains, the flesh of mighty men, and the flesh of horses and of those who sit on them, and the flesh of all men, both free and slave, and small and great."*

God summons every kind of scavenger bird to feast on the many of the world who decide to challenge the Lord exerting His authority over the earth, including the ten kings who die as we all die.

> *WEB Rev 19:19 I saw the beast, and the kings of the earth, and their armies, gathered together to make war against him who sat on the horse, and against his army.*

It is as David said:

NLT Ps 2:1 Why do the nations rage? Why do the people waste their time with futile plans?
NLT Ps 2:2 The kings of the earth prepare for battle; the rulers plot together against the LORD and against his anointed one.
NLT Ps 2:3 "Let us break their chains," they cry, "and free ourselves from this slavery."
NLT Ps 2:4 But the one who rules in heaven laughs. The Lord scoffs at them.
NLT Ps 2:5 Then in anger he rebukes them, terrifying them with his fierce fury.
NLT Ps 2:6 For the LORD declares, "I have placed my chosen king on the throne " in Jerusalem, my holy city.
NLT Ps 2:7 The king proclaims the LORD's decree: "The LORD said to me, 'You are my son. Today I have become your Father.
NLT Ps 2:8 Only ask, and I will give you the nations as your inheritance, the ends of the earth as your possession.
NLT Ps 2:9 You will break them with an iron rod and smash them like clay pots.'"
NLT Ps 2:10 Now then, you kings, act wisely! Be warned, you rulers of the earth!
NLT Ps 2:11 Serve the LORD with reverent fear, and rejoice with trembling.

NLT Ps 2:12 Submit to God's royal son, or he will become angry, and you will be destroyed in the midst of your pursuits—for his anger can flare up in an instant. But what joy for all who find protection in him!

NIV Ps 2:10 Therefore, you kings, be wise; be warned, you rulers of the earth.

NIV Ps 2:11 Serve the LORD with fear and rejoice with trembling.

NIV Ps 2:12 Kiss the Son, lest he be angry and you be destroyed in your way, for his wrath can flare up in a moment. Blessed are all who take refuge in him.

WEB Rev 19:20 The beast was taken, and with him the false prophet who worked the signs in his sight, with which he deceived those who had received the mark of the beast and those who worshiped his image. These two were thrown alive into the lake of fire that burns with sulfur.

It is as Isaiah predicted:

NRSV Isa 14:3 **Downfall of the King of Babylon**

When the LORD has given you rest from your pain and turmoil and the hard service with which you were made to serve, 4 you will take up this taunt against the king of Babylon:
How the oppressor has ceased!
How his insolence has ceased!
NRSV Isa 14:5 The LORD has broken the staff of the wicked,
the scepter of rulers,
NRSV Isa 14:6 that struck down the peoples in wrath
with unceasing blows,
that ruled the nations in anger
with unrelenting persecution.

The Lord is talking about Nimrod, the beast and antichrist. Although this is a prophetic taunt, it starts in the beginning and is talking to the essence of the beast which is Nimrod. Even the earth and the plants are at peace and joyful over his death, as we see below.

NRSV Isa 14:7 The whole earth is at rest and quiet;
they break forth into singing.
NRSV Isa 14:8 The cypresses exult over you,
the cedars of Lebanon, saying,
"Since you were laid low,

no one comes to cut us down."

NRSV Isa 14:9 *Sheol* (Hades, the realm of the disembodied—the dead) *beneath is stirred up*
to meet you when you come;
it rouses the shades (the disembodied souls—shadows) *to greet you,*
all who were leaders of the earth;
it raises from their thrones
all who were kings of the nations.
NRSV Isa 14:10 *All of them will speak*
and say to you:
"You too have become as weak as we!
You have become like us!'
NRSV Isa 14:11 *Your pomp is brought down to Sheol,*
and the sound of your harps;
maggots are the bed beneath you,
and worms are your covering.

NRSV Isa 14:12 *How you are fallen from heaven,*
O Day Star, son of Dawn!
How you are cut down to the ground,
you who laid the nations low!
NRSV Isa 14:13 *You said in your heart,*
"I will ascend to heaven;
I will raise my throne
above the stars of God;
I will sit on the mount of assembly
on the heights of Zaphon;
NRSV Isa 14:14 *I will ascend to the tops of the clouds,*
I will make myself like the Most High."
NRSV Isa 14:15 *But you are brought down to Sheol,*
to the depths of the Pit (the Abyss).
NRSV Isa 14:16 *Those who see you will stare at you,*
and ponder over you:
"Is this the man who made the earth tremble,
who shook kingdoms,
NRSV Isa 14:17 *who made the world like a desert*
and overthrew its cities,

who would not let his prisoners go home?"
NRSV Isa 14:18 *All the kings of the nations lie in glory,*
each in his own tomb;
NRSV Isa 14:19 *but you are cast out, away from your grave,*
like loathsome carrion (a decaying carcass),
clothed with the dead, those pierced by the sword,
who go down to the stones of the Pit,
like a corpse trampled underfoot.

There it is, Isaiah says it, Daniel and Revelation confirms it. The false prophet will make human sacrifices in the temple of God. Next, he will use the body parts of the dead to make an image of the beast. Then God has granted the power for him to give breath to that image and bring Nimrod back to life in that body/image (Rev 13:15). It will be as it says above. Nimrod, the first and last king of Babylon, will be cast out of the grave (the Abyss in Hades) and his disembodied soul will be clothed with the body parts of dead bodies which were sacrificed to bring him back to life.

Amp Isa 14:19 *But you are cast away from your tomb like a loathed growth or premature birth or an abominable branch [of the family] and like the raiment of the slain; and you are clothed with the slain, those thrust through with the sword, who go down to the stones of the pit [into which carcasses are thrown], like a dead body trodden underfoot.*

After Isaiah says, "you are clothed with the slain," the rest of that verse is not separate or new thoughts or statements but are additional descriptions of the same statement in order to emphasize his point of the raiment Nimrod's soul is clothed with when he comes back alive—dead body parts.

- The body you come back alive out of the grave with is made of *"Those thrust through with the sword."*
- "(Those) *who go down to the stones of the pit [into which carcasses are thrown]"* are what you come back to life in, so you can again walk the earth.
- *"(It is) like a dead body trodden underfoot"* that your soul is alive in, once you come out of the Abyss back to life.

It is for everyone to be resurrected from the dead. The Lord will give all a body for the second time in order to face judgment. Then all will be judged either fit to live on for eternity in the new heavens and the new earth, or to suffer a second death by being thrown alive into the lake of fire. The body all receive, is a body of the Lord's making. Not this body for the return of Nimrod! The false prophet creates it out of the parts of the dead he killed as a part of his evil magic to raise up the beast.

Solomon said that there is nothing new under the sun (Ecc 1:9). Mary Shelly's book, *Frankenstein,* was not as an original idea as she may have thought. She actually pulled her story down from the realm of the demonic, in the spiritual realm. Dr. Frankenstein would be the false prophet. His creation from the parts of dead bodies, Frankenstein, would be the beast, Nimrod. This act is such an affront and abomination to the Lord that he does not esteem the risen Nimrod as a person. That is why he is referred to as a beast. Also, as an "abomination" or "the abomination which causes desolation." On this occasion he is called the "desolater" (the one who caused the desolation).

This is the straw that breaks the camel's back. When this act is accomplished, the Holy Spirit withdraws from the earth because of it. Both in Daniel and in Revelation the body created for Nimrod is not given the dignity of being considered human. It is instead referred to as an "image" or the "image of the beast." In Genesis, the Lord referred to the giants, who were genetic distortions of the humans He made, as "men" because they were flesh and blood and would die like all men. But this body created out of dead human sacrifices, he calls an "image of the beast" who is able to "stand up", come to life in a body, and is able to kill all who do not worship him. Isaiah told us this constructed body is made with the dead, with parts from different decaying carcasses who were murdered for this purpose. Nimrod, who comes back from the dead, clothes his disembodied soul with a collection of body parts from the dead.

Note: At this time there is a doctor in the news who is looking for a country who will allow him to perform a total head transplant. China has agreed and with a 150 man team, work has started. China was the only nation of the ones he solicited who would allow him to perform such an atrocity. They have successfully performed the operation on animals and have transplanted the head of one corpse to the corpse of another taking 18 hours. They now have a volunteer who wants his head transplanted to the body of someone who is brain dead. They can transplant hearts and other body organs, now they will attempt to transplant a head to a different body. The stage is set for the evil magic of the false prophet.

Amp Da 9:27 *And he* (the false prophet/pope) *shall enter into a strong and firm covenant with the many for one week [seven years]. And in the midst of the week he shall cause the sacrifice and offering to cease [for the remaining three and one-half years]; and <u>upon the wing or pinnacle of abominations</u>* (at the height or climax of his abominations) *[shall come] one who makes desolate, until the full determined end is poured out on the desolator.*

That "one who makes desolate" is Nimrod who will rise up out of the Abyss to rule the globe.

NIV Da 12:11 *"From the time that the daily sacrifice is abolished and the abomination that causes desolation is set up, there will be 1,290 days.*
NIV Da 12:12 *Blessed is the one who waits for and reaches the end of the 1,335 days.*

1,290 days after the midpoint is 30 days after the 70th-7 comes to an end. In other words, the 70th-7 is complete 1,260 days after the midpoint, when the animal sacrifices are ordered to stop. It says here that the false prophet starts creating the body of the beast in the temple 30 days after the end of the last 7 of the 70-7's the Lord decreed.

Amp Rev 17:8 <u>*The beast that you saw [once] was, but [now] is no more, and he is going to come up out of the Abyss (the bottomless pit) and proceed to go to perdition.*</u> *And the inhabitants of the earth whose names have not been recorded in the Book of Life from the foundation of the world will be astonished when they look at the beast, <u>because he [once] was, but [now] is no more, and he is [yet] to come.</u>*
Amp Rev 17:9 *. . . The seven heads are seven hills upon which the woman is sitting;*
Amp Rev 17:10 *And they are also seven kings, five of whom have fallen, one still exists [and is reigning]; the other [the seventh]* (the popery starting with Leo III) *has not yet appeared, and when he does arrive, he must stay [but] a brief time.*
Amp Rev 17:11 *And as for the beast that [once] was, but now is no more, he [himself] is an eighth ruler (king, head), but he is of* (one of) *the seven and belongs to them, and he goes to perdition.*
NIV Rev 13:11 *Then I saw another beast, coming out of the earth. He had two horns like a lamb, but he spoke like a dragon.*
NIV Rev 13:12 *He exercised all the authority of the first beast on his behalf, and made the earth and its inhabitants worship the first beast, whose fatal wound had been healed.*
NIV Rev 13:13 *And he performed great and miraculous signs, even causing fire to come down from heaven to earth in full view of men.*

NIV Rev 13:14 *Because of the signs he was given power to do on behalf of the first beast, he deceived the inhabitants of the earth. He ordered them to set up an image in honor of the beast who was wounded by the sword and yet lived.*
NIV Rev 13:15 *He was given power to give breath to the image of the first beast, so that it could speak and cause all who refused to worship the image to be killed.*

NRSV Isa 14:19 *but you* (Nimrod) *are cast out, away from your grave, like loathsome carrion (a decaying carcass), clothed with the dead, those pierced by the sword . . .*

NIV Rev 17:17 *For God has put it into their hearts to accomplish his purpose by agreeing to give the beast their power to rule, until God's words are fulfilled.*

NIV Mt 24:15 *"So when you see standing in the holy place 'the abomination that causes desolation,' spoken of through the prophet Daniel—let the reader understand—*
NIV Mt 24:16 *then let those who are in Judea flee to the mountains.*
NIV Mt 24:17 *Let no one on the roof of his house go down to take anything out of the house.*
NIV Mt 24:18 *Let no one in the field go back to get his cloak.*

So, when you see come to life, this abomination able to stand upright, the image of the beast, Nimrod, who comes up from among the dead in the Abyss, flee! Jesus knows exactly what will take place and why. He is, after all, the one who opened the scroll and who is the Spirit of prophecy.

> *NRSV Isa 14:20* *You will not be joined with them in burial,*
> *because you have destroyed your land,*
> *you have killed your people.*
>
> *May the descendants of evildoers*
> *nevermore be named!*
> *NRSV Isa 14:21* *Prepare slaughter for his sons*
> *because of the guilt of their father.*
> *Let them never rise to possess the earth*
> *or cover the face of the world with cities.*

NRSV Isa 14:22 *I will rise up against them, says the LORD of hosts, and will cut off from Babylon name and remnant, offspring and posterity, says the LORD. ²³ And I will make it a possession of the hedgehog, and pools of water, and I will sweep it with the broom of destruction, says the LORD of hosts.*

NRSV Isa 14:24 **An Oracle concerning Assyria**
The LORD of hosts has sworn:
<u>*As I have designed,*</u>
<u>*so shall it be;*</u>
<u>*and as I have planned,*</u>
so shall it come to pass:
NRSV Isa 14:25 <u>I will break (crush) the Assyrian (Nimrod) in my land,</u>
<u>*and on my mountains trample him under foot;*</u>
<u>*his yoke shall be removed from them,*</u>
<u>*and his burden from their shoulders.*</u>
NRSV Isa 14:26 <u>This is the plan that is planned</u>
<u>*concerning the whole earth;*</u>
and this is the hand that is stretched out
over all the nations.
NRSV Isa 14:27 *For the LORD of hosts has planned,*
and who will annul it?
His hand is stretched out,
and who will turn it back?

NIV Rev 19:21 *The rest of them were killed with the sword that came out of the mouth of the rider on the horse, and all the birds gorged themselves on their flesh.*

NIV Heb 4:11 *Let us, therefore, make every effort to enter that rest, so that no one will fall by following their example of disobedience.*
NIV Heb 4:12 <u>For the word of God is living and active. Sharper than any double-edged sword, it penetrates even to dividing soul and spirit, joints and marrow; it judges the thoughts and attitudes of the heart.</u>
NIV Heb 4:13 *Nothing in all creation is hidden from God's sight. Everything is uncovered and laid bare before the eyes of him to whom we must give account.*

His words are like a double-edged sword, which cuts both ways. They bring life to those ready to reconcile with Him. However, they bring judgment to those who are determined to oppose God. The ten kings and all their armies are dead by the words which come out of the Lord's mouth. That is all the effort it takes on the part of the

Lord when it comes to answering the call of battle. Just as creation was spoken into existence, it only takes a word of judgment from the Lord for all His enemies and those who would oppose His authority over the earth, to perish. Everyone who gathers at Armageddon will die. It is that simple.

NLT Ps 2:1 Why do the nations rage? Why do the people waste their time with futile plans?
NLT Ps 2:2 The kings of the earth prepare for battle; the rulers plot together against the LORD and against his anointed one.
NLT Ps 2:3 "Let us break their chains," they cry, "and free ourselves from this slavery."
NLT Ps 2:4 But the one who rules in heaven laughs. The Lord scoffs at them.
NLT Ps 2:5 Then in anger he rebukes them, terrifying them with his fierce fury.

NLT Ps 2:9 You will break them with an iron rod and smash them like clay pots.'"
NLT Ps 2:10 Now then, you kings, act wisely! Be warned, you rulers of the earth!
NLT Ps 2:11 Serve the LORD with reverent fear, and rejoice with trembling.
NLT Ps 2:12 Submit to God's royal son, or he will become angry, and you will be destroyed in the midst of your pursuits— for his anger can flare up in an instant. But what joy for all who find protection in him!

In fact, the Lord did warn! We were told that after the second woe, no one repented from their evil ways.

NIV Rev 9:20 The rest of mankind that were not killed by these plagues (the second woe) *still did not repent of the work of their hands; they did not stop worshiping demons, and idols of gold, silver, bronze, stone and wood—idols that cannot see or hear or walk.*
NIV Rev 9:21 Nor did they repent of their murders, their magic arts, their sexual immorality or their thefts.

Then, before the third woe (which is death to all who come to the battle of Armageddon), the Lord warns those who would be seduced by the demonic words of the Devil (who is manifest on earth), the risen Nimrod, and the false prophet. In addition, hailstones weighing 100 pounds fall from the sky on the people. Natural disasters occur which change the topography of the earth resembling what it was before the flood.

NRSV Rev 16:13 And I saw three foul spirits like frogs coming from the mouth of the dragon, from the mouth of the beast, and from the mouth of the false prophet. ¹⁴ These are demonic spirits, performing signs, who go abroad to the kings of the whole world, to assemble them for battle on the great day of God the Almighty. ¹⁵ ("See, I am coming like a thief! Blessed is the one who stays awake and is clothed, not going about naked and exposed to shame.") ¹⁶ And they assembled them at the place that in Hebrew is called Harmagedon.

When Jesus comes as a thief, it will be against the global army that opposes Him. This battle has been the boast and dream of Nimrod who wants to go out in ultimate glory. He asked for this battle when he first lived on the earth.

"If I fall," Gilgamesh (Nimrod) says, "I will establish a name for myself. 'Gilgamesh is fallen,' they will say, 'in combat with terrible Huwawa (Yahweh).'"
"But if I win, they will say, Gilgamesh (Nimrod), the mighty vanquisher of Huwawa (Yahweh)!"

"Blessed is the one who stays awake and is clothed, not going about naked and exposed to shame." By this He is saying those who stay alert, alive and do not become naked or disembodied, they will be blessed. In other words, life on earth is hours away from becoming a paradise, it would be shameful or foolish to lose hope or be hypnotized by the call to battle with the Devil, the beast, and the false prophet. Do not fight me but stay away and you will live to see My 1,000 year reign.

Many do not heed the final warning of the Lord but are seduced by the defiant rebellion of Nimrod and will meet their end in that fateful battle.

> *WEB Rev 20:1 I saw an angel coming down out of heaven, having the key of the abyss and a great chain in his hand. ² He seized the dragon, the old serpent, which is the devil and Satan, who deceives the whole inhabited earth, and bound him for a thousand years, ³ and cast him into the abyss, and shut it, and sealed it over him, that he should deceive the nations no more, until the thousand years were finished. After this, he must be freed for a short time.*

Note: Some translations subtitle this part "The Thousand Years," starting with verse 20:1, making it the start of a new vision or subject after the vision of "The Rider on the White Horse." The vision of The Rider on the White Horse has as its subject the actual return (second coming) and the subduing of the earth by the Lord. This story is the seventh trumpet blast, which includes the ensuing battle of Armageddon, and the results of that battle. All of which leads into the next vision/subject which is the thousand year reign of Christ and the Kingdom of God as aptly titled, "The Thousand Years," which is not the conquering of it.

However, some of the translations that subtitle the beginning of each new subject on occasion, mis-divide one subject from the next. This is one of these occasions. Verse 20:1-3 are included as the beginning of the vision of the thousand years in some translations. Just like other occasions when this happens it is not a harmless mistake. It literally skews the timeline leaving it all but impossible to interpret.

In this case where certain translations incorrectly divide the subjects, they include chapter 20:1-3 as a part of the subtitle "The Thousand Years (reign of Christ)." To include those verses as the beginning of The Thousand Years gives the impression that the first resurrection (as described in verses 20:4-6) happens after the Devil is thrown into the Abyss. To do so totally contradicts every other vision that contains when the first resurrection takes place, completely skewing the timeline of the end times.

The true subject division (or the true beginning and end of the different visions) should end The Rider on the White Horse vision with the fate of the Devil, Rev 20:3. Then begin the vision of The Thousand Years with the first resurrection and return of Christ, starting with Rev 20:4. When divided this way, the book of Revelation maintains sound linear timelines within its four different narratives.

It is elementary that if the subject matter of the rider on the white horse is the return of the conquering Christ, it would include His subduing of the earth into His authority through the battle of Armageddon. Likewise, that subject would not be complete unless it reveals the results of that battle. The rider on the white horse is Jesus coming out to meet the nations at the battle of Armageddon. Not only are we foretold this event, but we are told its outcome. Everyone who shows up to fight Jesus die and are sent to the realm of the dead, Hades, awaiting the last day when they will be raised from the dead, judged and consequently face the second death of being thrown alive into the lake of fire. Next, the beast and the false prophet are not killed but captured, then thrown alive directly into the lake of fire for eternity.

Naturally, the conclusion should also give the fate of the Devil who also was the instigator and organizer of this battle and was present. Otherwise this subject would not be complete in its information. Indeed it does, it tells us he is bound and locked in the Abyss for a thousand years. And, like Nimrod's return, it tells us that (after the 1,000 years) he is permitted to leave the Abyss, for a time, on his way to the lake of fire, in order to complete the plans of God.

Ending it after verse 20:3 makes the subject of the rider on the white horse complete. It is only after that conclusion does it start a new vision with its new subject. That new subject is not the return and subjection of the world under His authority, but the reign of His established Kingdom. However, knowing that this is a new vision with a new subject, we understand that it has its own starting point with its own timeline.

This vision of the rider on the white horse now brings us to the aftermath and conclusion of the battle of Armageddon and the victory of the Lord on His white horse as described in verses 20:1-3 (above). To once again sum it up, all the people who showed up for battle died. Nimrod (the beast) and the false prophet had already served their time in Hades, even in the Abyss. For them, they suffer the second death of being thrown alive into the lake of fire. The Devil who has been manifest in the earth for 3-1/2 years is thrown into the Abyss of Hades. He does not die or become disembodied like those who lie dead while the scavenger birds feast upon their flesh. His body is not made of flesh and blood. His body is made of spiritual matter. Nevertheless, he is confined in the Abyss for the length of the 1,000 years reign of the Lord.

During the thousand year reign of Christ, men will not be influenced by the Devil. They will also live in a time in which the curse of the four horsemen has been lifted by the Lord. The human spirit had been corrupted by the Devil in the Garden, and as a result it will remain so until the last day. Notwithstanding that spiritual condition, the Devil will not be in the earth influencing and tempting the mortal men who live. Nor will he be present before God railing against the people, pointing out their sins and petitioning God for them to pay for their sins by their death. However, verse 3 (above) tells us when the 1,000 years are finished, he must be let loose in the earth again in order to finish the plan of God; as laid out in the scroll with seven seals.

CHAPTER 4

The Thousand Years

Although in the overall timeline of the entire narrative, the thousand year reign obviously follows the return of Christ and His conquering of the world. However, the story of the thousand year reign can choose as its starting point the place which makes sense of it all. That starting point of this new story is when the Lord and His entourage gather in the sky and come down to the earth with Him. The entourage gathered with Him includes those He resurrects from the dead and those who had endured the great tribulation without coming off of their testimony, not worshiping the beast, or taking His mark.

It is only after the victory of the battle of Armageddon that His Kingdom of a thousand years will begin, however, His return with His entourage and the New Jerusalem happens before the final battle of Armageddon. The return of Christ is the natural beginning of this new subject, the thousand years. Again, how does that return begin? This story begins with Jesus gathering His celestial humans to follow Him down to the earth from the sky. This next story or vision subtitled "The Thousand Years" starts with verse 20:4 (below).

> WEB Rev 20:4 *I saw thrones, and they sat on them, and judgment was given to them. I saw the souls of those who had been beheaded for the testimony of Jesus, and for the word of God, and such as didn't worship the beast nor his image, and didn't receive the mark on their forehead and on their hand. They lived and reigned with Christ for a thousand years.*

There are three groups of people mentioned above:

1) (NIV) "I saw thrones on which were seated those who had been given authority to judge." This first group are those who have already received their celestial

bodies. Among this group are; **A)** the 144,000; **B)** those taken up in the rapture; **C)** those starting with Stephen up to, but not including those taken in the rapture, who are in union with Christ, and do not taste death, but become celestial humans before the hearts of their mortal bodies stopped beating.

2)   "And I saw the souls of those who had been beheaded because of their testimony for Jesus and because of the word of God. They had not worshiped the beast or his image and had not received his mark on their foreheads or their hands. They came to life and reigned with Christ a thousand years." These are those who participate in the first resurrection. They are the great multitude. They were killed in the great tribulation, and only those killed in the great tribulation take part in the first resurrection.

Included in this group are those who survived the great tribulation and had lived through it with the same integrity as the others who had died in it. They did not come off their testimony in Christ. Neither did they worship the beast, or take his mark. Both, those who were killed but are resurrected, and those who endured but remained alive, are, at the same time, raptured to meet Jesus in the sky while receiving their celestial bodies.

This is the occasion that Paul was describing in his letter to the Thessalonians. Many believe he is speaking of the rapture that happens the day the great tribulation begins. That is not the case. Paul is teaching about this occasion in verse 20:4 (above), which is the first resurrection, and precedes the second coming of Christ. Paul states clearly that his subject is the Lord's coming. That is why there is no focus on the first rapture which takes place the day the two witnesses are called up to heaven, and the tribulation begins.

NRSV 1Th 4:13 But we do not want you to be uninformed, brothers and sisters, [18] about those who have died, [19] so that you may not grieve as others do who have no hope. [14] For since we believe that Jesus died and rose again, even so, through Jesus, God will bring with him those who have died.

Above where it states, "*through Jesus, God will bring with him those who have died.*" Paul is talking about those before the great tribulation whose bodies died while they were in union with Christ but did not experience death and had already become celestial humans. This includes those who were caught up in the first rapture and became celestial humans. When He returns, He will bring those with Him, among others that Paul describes below.

NRSV 1Th 4:15 For this we declare to you by the word of the Lord, that we who are alive, who are <u>left until the coming of the Lord,</u> will by no means precede those who have died. ¹⁶ For the Lord himself, with a cry of command, with the archangel's call and with the sound of God's trumpet, will descend from heaven, <u>and the dead in Christ will rise first.</u>

Concerning the above in verse 15 and 16, this is called the first resurrection. These dead in Christ are those who died in the great tribulation and as disembodied souls went to the paradisiacal place in Hades, known also as Abraham's bosom. As a result of the global desolation (the absence of the presence of God) during the great tribulation, those who die in it, do taste death, they do become disembodied. Those who die in the great tribulation will rise to life at the first resurrection just as the many patriarchs who came out of their tombs after Jesus gave up His Spirit (Mt 27:50-54). Again, they do become disembodied and sent to the realm of the dead. But before the return of Christ they are resurrected by being given a celestial body. They are not saved by relationship, or by deeds, but by their profession. It is through proving their profession of faith true by standing behind it even unto death. However, that was not the case formerly, before the great tribulation:

Amp Jn 11:26 And <u>whoever continues to live</u> and believes in (has faith in, cleaves to, and relies on) Me <u>shall never [actually] die at all.</u> Do you believe this?

And again:

Amp Jn 5:24 I assure you, most solemnly I tell you, the person whose ears are open to My words [who listens to My message] and believes and trusts in and clings to and relies on Him Who sent Me has (possesses now) eternal life. <u>And he does not come into</u>

judgment [does not incur sentence of judgment, will not come under condemnation], but he has already passed over out of death into life.

Those in union with Christ who died before the tribulation and after the cross never experienced (even for a moment) a state of disembodiment, which is the state of death. Unfortunately, many Christians do not live in union with Christ; meaning to die to self by no longer living for their own aspirations, agendas, and goals, but like Paul, live to carry out every prompting of the Holy Spirit. To live in this manner has nothing to do with doing right or wrong or being charitable. This status is based not on deeds but relationship—how you relate to Christ through His Spirit (the Holy Spirit).

Spiritual union is actually the New Covenant relationship that gives the promise that we will never die—never experience death—that we will translate into celestial humans possessing celestial bodies before our mortal bodies become dead and our heart stops beating.

The rest who do good, love and obey God's laws while living for their own aspirations, agendas and goals, like the Jews, will die becoming disembodied, assigned to the paradisiacal place of Hades, and will be judged as sheep on the last day. They will be rewarded with eternal life, gaining a celestial body at that time because of their good deeds. However, that does not qualify one to attain the benefit of never tasting death that the New Covenant promises. It is not by deeds but through the relationship, the relationship of *spiritual union* with Christ that one receives the promise of the New Covenant.

NRSV 1Th 4:17 *Then we who are alive, who are left, will be caught up in the clouds together with them* (who were just resurrected) *to meet the Lord in the air; and so we will be with the Lord forever.* ¹⁸ *Therefore encourage one another with these words.*

When the dead are risen after the great tribulation it will horrify the entire world. They are the hundreds of millions that they have killed over the previous 3-1/2 years. Then some undetermined time after they have risen from the dead, walking the earth once again, and together (with those faithful) who are alive, will rise up to meet Jesus in the sky above the earth; just before He descends with them all.

NRSV 1Th 5:1 Now concerning the times and the seasons, brothers and sisters, you do not need to have anything written to you. ² For you yourselves know very well that the day of the Lord will come like a thief in the night. ³ When they say, "There is peace and security," then sudden destruction will come upon them, as labor pains come upon a pregnant woman, and there will be no escape!

Paul is referring to when the great tribulation ends, and the wrath of God is poured out on the world. Having killed most of the Christians they will think they have a perfect world. Acceptance without conformity, the religion and way of Cain, will rule the day. Then the sky opens up and Jesus is visible from horizon to horizon poised to come down, then suddenly the judgment of five trumpet blasts, including one woe, will befall the earth in a day.

NRSV 1Th 5:4 But you, beloved, are not in darkness, for that day to surprise you like a thief; ⁵ for you are all children of light and children of the day; we are not of the night or of darkness. ⁶ So then let us not fall asleep as others do, but let us keep awake and be sober; ⁷ for those who sleep sleep at night, and those who are drunk get drunk at night. ⁸ But since we belong to the day, let us be sober, and put on the breastplate of faith and love, and for a helmet the hope of salvation. ⁹ For God has destined us not for wrath but for obtaining salvation through our Lord Jesus Christ, ¹⁰ who died for us, so that whether we are awake or asleep we may live with him. ¹¹ Therefore encourage one another and build up each other, as indeed you are doing.

WEB Rev 20:5 The rest of the dead didn't live until the thousand years were finished. This is the first resurrection. ⁶ Blessed and holy is he who has part in the first resurrection. Over these, the second death has no power, but they will be priests of God and of Christ, and will reign with him one thousand years.

3) "The rest of the dead didn't live until the thousand years were finished."

Meaning, they did not come back to life being clothed once again in a body until the last day. This third group mentioned here are the rest of the people who have lived and died on planet earth from the beginning. After the thousand year reign of Christ, the last day will come. That day is also known as "the day of the Lord."

Amp 2Pe 3:7 But by the same word the present heavens and <u>earth have been stored up (reserved) for fire, being kept until the day of judgment and destruction of the ungodly people.</u>

Amp 2Pe 3:10 But the day of the Lord will come like a thief, and then the heavens will vanish (pass away) with a thunderous crash, and the [material] elements [of the universe] will be dissolved with fire, and the earth and the works that are upon it will be burned up.

Amp 2Pe 3:11 Since all these things are thus in the process of being dissolved, what kind of person ought [each of] you to be [in the meanwhile] in consecrated and holy behavior and devout and godly qualities,

Amp 2Pe 3:12 While you wait and earnestly long for (expect and hasten) the coming of the day of God by reason of which <u>the flaming heavens will be dissolved, and the [material] elements [of the universe] will flare and melt with fire?</u>

Amp 2Pe 3:13 But we look for <u>new heavens and a new earth according to His promise, in which righteousness (uprightness, freedom from sin, and right standing with God) is to abide.</u>

All will be resurrected from the dead since the beginning of the earth until its last day, then face God for judgment. The sheep and goats will be separated from each other while being judged by how they conducted themselves while in the body. The sheep will go onto eternal life as celestial humans. However, they will not have the stature of those who already became celestial humans and who do not at that time face judgment, but co-judge with the Lord. Nor will the last day sheep reign with Christ for 1,000 years as His ministers to the mortal humans. The celestial humans before them will live in the New Jerusalem. They will speak to the Lord face to face and be His ministers to the mortal humans. Nevertheless, as David said:

Amp Ps 84:10 For a day in Your courts is better than a thousand [anywhere else]; I would rather be a doorkeeper and stand at the threshold in the house of my God than to dwell [at ease] in the tents of wickedness.

As for the goats, the ones found wanting, they will be thrown alive into the lake of fire suffering a second but eternal death. Then the realm of the dead will likewise be thrown into the lake of fire. For it will not serve any purpose anymore. No longer will there be any dead and dying which await the judgment of God.

CHAPTER 5

Satan's Doom

John is now being shown Satan's end, his doom. In the previous vision John was shown the results of the battle of Armageddon. Satan was manifest on the earth after being thrown out of the heavenly realm, and specifically from the presence of God. He became visible in that the people on the earth could see his form. Along with the false prophet and the beast, the Devil seduced the people of the world to fight against the Lord and His host who now had come down to the earth in the New Jerusalem. After the battle of Armageddon, an angel with heavy chains bound Satan and threw him into the bottomless pit, the Abyss, locking him away. However, this is not his final doom because we were told he would be set free after 1,000 years.

The imprisonment of the Devil in the Abyss is unlike the beast, and the false prophet of whom John was told was thrown alive into the lake of fire. We have come to the end of any subject's story once he has been thrown alive into the lake of fire suffering a second death. There is no reprieve, hope, or life after arriving at this destination.

The first death confining you to Hades, or the Abyss within it, are temporal places, imprisoning both the dead and the fallen celestial beings the Lord has judged. They are not forever. Death itself is temporal in the sense that death (or the state of death) will be no more, after the last day. Likewise, Hades and the realm of the dead will be emptied and have no purpose after all have risen back to life. Death will then be cast into the eternal fire as will the realm of Hades. Evil will be thrown into the fire along with all who possess that spirit.

However, as damning as his destination is, the Abyss is not a permanent prison. Again, the antichrist and false prophet have met their final end, suffering the second death of being thrown alive into the lake of fire, but it is not so for the Devil—not yet. We see how this is true below:

> *WEB Rev 20:7 And after the thousand years, Satan will be released from his prison, 8 and he will come out to deceive the nations which are in the four corners of the earth, Gog and Magog, to gather them together to the war; the number of whom is as the sand of the sea. 9a They went up over the width of the earth, and surrounded the camp of the saints, and the beloved city.*

Gog and Magog, can also be translated as Gog from (the land of) Gog.

Note: The following is an explanation of the confusions surrounding where the Gog-Magog battle fits on the timeline of Biblical prophecy. There is a school of thought which places the battle of Gog-Magog before the 1,000 year reign of Christ and then makes the quantum leap that therefore it is in fact the battle of Armageddon. However, we are clearly told in the verses above that the battle of Armageddon happens as a matter of the Lord conquering the kingdom of the beast so as to make Himself the King and Lord of the entire globe. This is a position that the beast possesses when Jesus returns to the earth and has to be taken from him. Then equally as clear we are told that the battle of Gog-Magog happens after the 1,000 year reign of Christ in verse 20:7 (above).

This confusion can be blamed, once again, on the choice of paragraph division by the translators (or lack of paragraph division). In the book of Ezekiel (38:1-39:20), he has a vision describing the battle of Gog-Magog. This prophecy occurs after the 1,000 year reign of Christ, as we learned above in verses 7-8. The problem is that there should be a paragraph division at the end of verse 20 in Ezekiel because the subject changes from, (1) how in the end God will deal with the nations who come against His people, to (2) why Israel has been treated by God the way they have been throughout history.

However, without a paragraph separation after verse 20, what follows appears to be the conclusion of what is spoken from verses 38:1-39:20. When verses 39:21-29 are read as part of what is described in verses 38:1-39:20, then it places the battle of Gog-Magog before the 1,000 year reign of Christ. This, in turn, misleads people into concluding that the battle of Gog-Magog is the battle of Armageddon.

Therefore, proper place for the subject division is when God finishes speaking about how, in the end, God will deal with the nations who come against His people at verse 39:20. Then there should be a new paragraph to signify a new subject starting with verse 39:21. That new subject is, why Israel has been treated by God the way they have been throughout history. This preserves the timeline and keeps everything in its proper perspective.

The next question has to be asked: Why?

Why is this battle with Gog—Magog necessary? Why after defeating all evil in the world and arresting the source of it, and after a thousand years of peaceful rule by the Lord of lords does the Lord need to unleash the Devil and his evil to seduce the world into rebellion one more time? Also, who is this Gog—Magog in the first place?

Is this final battle fought to give the Devil his last stand and infamous glory? This is not the answer because in every step of the way, as soon as the Devil has served his usefulness in God carrying out His plan, the Devil is put down right away. Like for example, his role in Job's personal tribulations. As soon as Job was finished being tested by God and they have their encounter (God and Job), the Devil is no longer a part of the story and not mentioned again.

Jesus paid the price for sin itself and it was forgiven by God. Eventually, there becomes no need for the Devil to have access to the throne of God in heaven, constantly railing against the saints, reminding God of our sins. As a result, that aspect of his usefulness in God's plan being null and void, the Devil is overpowered and cast out of heaven to the earth along with his demons. Then we see after his usefulness of empowering his human agents on the earth to war against the saints has served its purposes, he is immediately cast into the Abyss where he could have no effect in the world.

It stands to reason that it is for the purposes of God to be accomplished that the Devil would have one more shot at the world. The question becomes, what is the purpose that unleashing such evil will serve good?

The Devil, like all who entered the Abyss, is able to rise from it to face final judgment. The beast (Nimrod) and the false prophet are given a layover (if you will) of seven years in the earth from the time they rise from the Abyss, until their sentence of the lake of fire begins. This was to fulfill the purposes of God. The Devil also will have a short time period on the earth after he is released from the Abyss and before he goes on to the lake of fire.

We know the beast had seven years, however, all we know about the Devil is that it is a "short time" or a "little season." It is not typical for this to happen, in fact it is the exception. It is for God's purposes of redeeming the redeemable, if you will; separating the wheat from the tare. God will be finishing His plan that He decreed in the Garden to Adam, Eve, and the Devil.

God will be sifting one last time to separate the offspring of the Devil from the offspring of Eve's as a part of the final harvest of the earth. The choice of each individual person to join in attacking God's people with the Devil, or to not attack the Lord and His people, will determine which line of offspring every individual of the earth will identify with. This happens before the last day and final judgment when the earth will be no more, neither will there be any mortal humans. It will be the last chance in a valley of decision which will determine each individual's destination for eternity.

We need to remember that the power of the four horsemen was first issued to the Devil and then he endowed his human agents with it. For 1,000 years (during the reign of Christ) that power and spirit has been deprived from having access to the earth. All who possess it have been thrown alive into the lake of fire or into the Abyss waiting to be judged and thrown alive into the lake of fire. The source of it (the Devil), was merely locked away so as not to have an influence with it in the world. However, as with the beast (Nimrod) and the false prophet, God grants this time on purpose.

His purpose is no longer to give that power to those in the world so that they may punish God's own people and thereby purify them, as was the case of the great tribulation. His chosen people have already been purified and live in harmony with Him, as He has taken up residence with His people. This is verified by the fact that when Gog-Magog do attack, they harm not one single person of the Lord's. Additionally, it is the Lord Himself who defeats them before they are able to harm anyone. His people need not even be afraid or have to defend themselves or have to hide behind the walls of a city. No, unleashing this power on the earth once again is not for the purpose to test the people of God, but to separate the redeemable from among the other mortals still living in the earth.

All of God's people already have supernatural or celestial bodies suitable to live in the supernatural world to come. That is with the exception of those people in Israel who live in their mortal bodies. Again, they have received God's Spirit in them and live in *spiritual union* with Him.

Then, there are people left in the world who live with their mortal bodies and who had taken the mark of the beast and worshiped the image of the beast. As well, there are their children. It is about 25 to 30 generations (1,000 years) since the kingdom of darkness fell. The nations they live in have been healed by the celestial humans of the King (Jesus) from the city, the New Jerusalem. It has become mandatory for these nations to not only serve Israel, but to pay homage to them with their resources. If not, the King will cause it to stop raining in their nation resulting in droughts, until they submit. How much resistance the nations will put up against these sanctions, if any, is not revealed through prophecy. The only thing which is revealed is that if they resist by noncompliance there are consequences.

NIV Eze 38:4 I will turn you around, put hooks in your jaws and bring you out with your whole army . . .

We do know, however, that they will lack the power, inspiration, and authority to organize a collective resistance or army to openly rebel. The power and authority (the first of the four horsemen) to do so left the earth with the Devil and is safely locked away with him in the Abyss. When he returns, he will still obviously have that power and use it to enlist Gog-Magog and the nations to have one last final battle with the Lord.

After having used the evil powers of the earth to sift, discipline, and punish the people He had made for Himself, the Lord has ordained this time to show all history and all of heaven and earth that His favor and protection of His people is absolute. His word is holy, and irrevocable (Praise God!). And through this final battle with Gog—Magog, the Lord will also show as great as an assembly can be, it is no use to come against His people. He Himself will protect them.

After this battle of Gog—Magog everything which stands against the will of God both in the spiritual realm and the natural will have had expression and will have been addressed, and then finally judged. Nothing swept under the carpet. Nothing has not been allowed to show experientially the true motives of the heart.

This test of letting the Devil loose and the gathering of the nations against God and his people, Israel, is as stated not a test to purify God's people. It is rather a test for the balance of the living. The Lord is about to decide who is fit, loyal, and truly desires to submit to the will of God on the last day. Everyone has had their choice as to which side their heart desires. The Lord has let the remainder of mortal men live under His rule for 1,000 years. They have had a taste to know what that is like. Now, before the last day when the Lord decides who is right for being in His Kingdom for eternity, He gives the last of mortal men a choice to see what is in their hearts. He does this by letting the Devil loose and letting him use that power to organize an army of those who would be against God.

God is going to let them do no harm, but to give them leave to choose against His Kingdom. It's like, before we do this Kingdom thing for eternity, you mortals who were left, can have one more chance to show if you would rebel or reject God. That is, after you have had a taste of what it's like for 1,000 years and before it becomes permanent. It is also likened to Abraham while called to sacrifice his son Isaac.

Abraham was tested to see if he would obey God. He had Isaac bound on the altar and as he began his downward stroke to plunge the knife into his son's chest, an angel of the Lord stopped him. It was Abraham's committed intent and motive that God wanted experiential proof of. It is the same with all of the mortal men in the earth except Israel. They are tested through the Devil and allowed to want to destroy Israel. After they have gathered together with their weapons and after they surround Israel, they have shown, experientially, the intents and motives of their hearts. Just as with Abraham, once this has occurred, the Lord does not allow them to follow through, but destroys them after they have shown what is truly in their hearts.

This is the purpose that the Devil was released from the Abyss for, and the battle of God-Magog was allowed to happen. The balance of the humans who do not join that battle will have opportunity on the last day to be declared sheep and receive eternal life. The rest who participated are thrown alive into the lake of fire once they have been resurrected for judgment.

WEB Pr 26:11 As a dog that returns to his vomit, so is a fool who repeats his folly.

Gog-Magog

A Prophecy Against Gog

NIV Eze 38:1 The word of the LORD came to me:

NIV Eze 38:2 "Son of man, set your face against Gog, of the land of Magog, the chief prince of Meshech and Tubal; prophesy against him

NIV Eze 38:3 and say: 'This is what the Sovereign LORD says: I am against you, O Gog, chief prince of Meshech and Tubal.

Who is Gog and Magog? There is not much information about them in the Bible. Here we will put together all that is known about them. We do know their origin. It says of Gog's lineage it comes from Reuben, the first born of Jacob (Israel):

WEB 1Ch 5:3 the sons of Reuben the firstborn of Israel: Hanoch, Pallu, Hezron, and Carmi. ⁴ The sons of Joel: Shemaiah his son, <u>Gog</u> his son, Shimei his son, ⁵ Micah his son, Reaiah his son, Baal his son, ⁶ and Beerah his son, whom Tilgath Pilneser king of Assyria carried away captive. He was prince of the Reubenites.

The Jewish encyclopedia says:

> <u>Gog is the leader of the seventy-two nations of the world, minus one (Israel)</u>, and makes war against the Most High; he is smitten down by God. Armilus rises as the last enemy of God and Israel.[3]

The above explains why, when it says:

Amp Rev 20:8 And he will go forth to deceive and seduce and <u>lead astray the nations which are in the four quarters of the earth—Gog and Magog</u>—to muster them for war; their number is like the sand of the sea.

Note: The count of nations and languages in Genesis chapter 10 is 70. Some early Christian sources reflect 72 nations and languages. There are a variety of opinions as to why there is a difference. However, this study goes by the tally given in Genesis chapter 10, and for the sake of staying on point we will not explore the differences.

In calling the nations Gog-Magog (or Gog, the land of Gog), Revelation (above) is calling all the nations of the world and their territories (the four quarters of the earth), Gog-Magog (except Israel). In antiquity, Gog is the leader of the 70 nations of the world, minus 1, after God disbursed them to the four corners of the earth; while confusing their languages after the Tower of Babel. That human leader was Nimrod, but ultimately it is the Devil and those nations are his offspring. All the people of those nations defied God and followed Nimrod. This was so they might do as they willed and be protected by Nimrod, while not suffering consequences from God.

When this rebellion with Nimrod and the 70 nations occurred, is when it all began! This is when the final judgment was decreed by God and the four horsemen were released; changing life on earth forever. It was then that life on earth became a hostile and unsafe place to live. Although there are currently 195 nations in the world, except Israel, they are all born from the three sons of Noah and have their essence from the 70 nations who rebelled against God. Even the Christians (in general) are from the line of the offspring of the Devil. They are those of the offspring of the Devil who are redeemable having had a spiritual rebirth becoming children of God, and no longer of the line of the offspring of the Devil. However, the age of the Church has ended before the 1,000 year reign of Christ and is no more, after having been utterly destroyed.

The only trace of the Church and its age during the 1,000 year reign is the bride of Christ who are the celestial humans that co-reign with Christ from the New Jerusalem. The Church Age is a window which becomes closed before the return of Christ, with all traces of it on mortal earth either ashes, or the smoke of her burning rising to eternity. Christianity (the Church) is not a part of the 1,000 year reign. On the last day of the great tribulation, never will a Christian ever die again. At the first resurrection and its ensuing rapture, turning its recipients into celestial humans who meet Jesus in the sky, the final numbers of those who are reconciled with God as the Church, will have been attained. All the Christians of the earth will then have met their end, whatever it is, and the mortal Church on earth will never again exist.

Amp Rev 18:22 *And the sound of harpists and minstrels and flute players and trumpeters shall never again be heard in you, and no skilled artisan of any craft shall ever again be found in you, and the sound of the millstone shall never again be heard in you.*

Amp Rev 18:23 *And never again shall the light of a lamp shine in you, and the voice of bridegroom and bride shall never be heard in you again; for your businessmen were the great and prominent men of the earth, and by your magic spells and poisonous charm all nations were led astray (seduced and deluded).*

Amp Rev 18:24 *And in her was found the blood of prophets and of saints, and of all those who have been slain (slaughtered) on earth.*

Amp Rev 19:1 *AFTER THIS I heard what sounded like a mighty shout of a great crowd in heaven, exclaiming, Hallelujah (praise the Lord)! Salvation and glory (splendor and majesty) and power (dominion and authority) [belong] to our God!*

Amp Rev 19:2 *Because His judgments (His condemnation and punishment, His sentences of doom) are true and sound and just and upright. He has judged (convicted, pronounced sentence, and doomed) the great and notorious harlot (idolatress) who corrupted and demoralized and poisoned the earth with her lewdness and adultery (idolatry). And He has avenged (visited on her the penalty for) the blood of His servants at her hand.*

Amp Rev 19:3 *And again they shouted, Hallelujah (praise the Lord)! The smoke of her [burning] shall continue to ascend forever and ever (through the eternities of the eternities).*

As a result, there is Israel and then all the other nations with the redeemed Christians having been extracted out. The only hope to be reconciled with God during the 1,000 year reign of Christ lies in either becoming a citizen of Israel (which under the Lord's instruction, Israel welcomes all to do), or to **1)** comply with the Lord as citizens of the nations, and **2)** not join the nations when led by the Devil to depose the Lord at the end of the 1,000 years.

In calling all the nations Gog-Magog, the circumstances of humanity (save Israel) are right back at the beginning and root of when it all happened soon after the flood. Out of the 70 nations of mortal humans there is one nation, Israel and its 12 tribes, whose sovereign is the Lord, and whose people are the line of offspring of the woman clothed with the sun, crowned with the twelve stars, Eve.

So, when it says the Devil will lead astray the nations spread out in the four corners of the earth—Gog-Magog (or Gog from the land of Gog), it is talking about all the nations who are of the line of the offspring of the Devil. That is except for Israel, who is from a different but opposing line of offspring—the Lord's (Eve's). That is why Revelation is calling all the nations in every corner of the earth—Gog-Magog (or Gog from the land of Gog).

NIV Rev 6:2 I looked, and there before me was a white horse! <u>Its rider held a bow, and he was given a crown, and he rode out as a conqueror bent on conquest.</u>

Perhaps this leader, Gog, is the first of the four horsemen, the celestial angels of destruction and conquest. Or more likely he adopts that spirit power of conquest from the same source as Nimrod did—the Devil and the first of the four horsemen. There is much in extra Biblical literature which accredits many of the traits given Nimrod and the Assyrian to Gog. That is even down to calling them both the antichrist, thus promoting the idea that the battle of Gog-Magog is synonymous with the battle of Armageddon.

Nimrod and Gog both have the same role, however, at different times. That role is to define the chasm between the two different lines of offspring. Through the enmity between them, it causes the people to clearly expose the spirit of their hearts when they decide which line of offspring they identify with and give themselves over to. Nevertheless, they both, Nimrod and Gog, have their origin in the rebellion against God after the flood.

When Jesus responded to Peter He said, "get behind me Satan!" Jesus was not name calling, but with His insight Jesus was talking to the very essence of the spirit behind Peter's words. To call the nations and those who gather them together in rebellion against the Lord at the end of time, "Gog-Magog," the Lord is speaking to the spirit of rebellion in its essence, piercing right through to its origin. To remove a tree, the Lord pulls it up by its roots and does not address it by cutting it off and leaving a stump.

It says of Magog that he is a son of Japheth, who was the son of Noah:

NIV Ge 10:2 The sons of Japheth: Gomer, <u>Magog</u>, Madai, Javan, Tubal, Meshech and Tiras.

Amp Ge 10:5 <u>From these the coastland peoples spread.</u> [These are the sons of Japheth] in their lands, each with his own language, by their families within their nations.

Here are some of the traditions of who Gog-Magog are in different cultures:

As previously mentioned, it is interpreted by some that it is Gog of Magog or Gog of the land of Gog, believing Magog has become a land or kingdom. There are many different things written about these two names. They are thought of as having come from the area of Russia and the Ukraine. Around the Caucasus mountain range and Black Sea. The Caucasus Mountains, which are the highest in Europe, separate the Black Sea from the Caspian Sea. In that area through the mountains was a major trade route especially for silk which joined Europe and Asia.

This is why Gog—Magog are thought of as being the Russians. However, it says that when they come to attack Israel they are said to come from the extreme north. And that the nations of the four quarters of the earth will join them. That does not mean that they are from that area, but it does say that they rally the nations to the extreme north in order to march on Israel. It must be factored in that when Jesus comes back to the earth, the entire topography of the earth changes. The islands will be no more, the mountains will be leveled, including the Caucasus Mountains that separate the Black and Caspian seas. Likewise, the continents will shift and some of the seas will dry up. So, what lies to the extreme north of Israel now, most likely will be something entirely different during and after the 1,000 year reign of Christ, when Gog-Magog attacks.

They are recorded as fierce warring barbarians. To the Greeks they are a mythical people. Recorded in Homer's Odyssey, they can be connected with a people as living beyond the ocean waters in a land of fog and darkness at the edge of the world before the entrance of Hades.

It is believed in Arabic literature that Alexander the Great built a wall to shut them off from the rest of the world. Some have confused this wall with the Great Wall of China. However, it was written that it was a wall which reached the mountain tops made of iron brick with molten brass as mortar. And as a sign of the day of judgment this wall will be broken.

Again, these barbarians in Arabic literature record them as small, only the size of half a man. However, very ferocious having claws instead of nails; lion like teeth; the jaw of a camel; and their body completely covered with hair. Their ears are so large they use one for a bed to sleep on and the other to cover themselves. They live on fish miraculously provided. They resemble animals in their habits and are considered beasts. Where they habitat they ravage the country, devouring everything green, and this is the reason Alexander was asked to build a wall. In their literature it is said when they come to attack Jerusalem and Israel they will devour everything in their path, eating everyone they meet, even corpses, and every green thing. They will cross the Sea of Galilee on their way on dry ground because they will drink its water dry.

In England they are thought of as giants who are guardians of the city of London. On the 2nd Saturday of November each year there is a parade in honor of them called, "The Lord Mayor's Show."

Main article: GogMagog (folklore)

Despite their generally negative depiction in the Bible, Lord Mayors of the City of London carry images of Gog and Magog (depicted as giants) in a traditional procession in the Lord Mayor's Show. According to the tradition, the giants Gog and Magog are guardians of the City of London, and images of them have been carried in the Lord Mayor's Show since the days of King Henry V. The Lord Mayor's procession takes place each year on the second Saturday of November.

The Lord Mayor's account of Gog and Magog says that the Roman Emperor Diocletian had thirty-three wicked daughters. He found thirty-three husbands for them to curb their wicked ways; they chafed at this, and under the leadership of the eldest sister, Alba, they murdered their husbands. For this crime they were set adrift at sea; they washed ashore on a windswept island, which they named "Albion"—after Alba. (*Albon is the oldest name given for the island of Great Britain*) Here they coupled with demons and gave birth to a race of giants, whose descendants included Gog and Magog.

An even older British connection to Gog and Magog appears in Geoffrey of Monmouth's influential 12th century Historia Regum Britanniae, which states that Goemagot was a giant slain by the eponymous Cornish hero Corin or Corineus. The tale figures in the body of unlikely lore that has Britain settled by the Trojan soldier Brutus and other fleeing heroes from the Trojan War. Corineus supposedly slew the giant by throwing him into the sea near Plymouth: Richard Carew notes the presence of chalk figures carved on Plymouth Hoe in his time. Wace (Roman de Brut), Layamon (Layamon's Brut) (who calls the giant Goemagog), and other chroniclers retell the story, which was picked up by later poets and romanciers. John Milton's History of Britain gives this version:

The Island, not yet Britain, but Albion, was in a manner desert and inhospitable, kept only by a remnant of Giants, whose excessive Force and Tyrannie had consumed the rest. Them Brutus destroies, and to his people divides the land, which, with some reference to his own name, he thenceforth calls Britain. To Corineus, Cornwall, as now we call it, fell by lot; the rather by him lik't, for that the hugest Giants in Rocks and Caves were said to lurk still there; which kind of Monsters to deal with was his old exercise.

And heer, with leave bespok'n to recite a grand fable, though dignify'd by our best Poets: While Brutus, on a certain Festival day, solemnly kept on that shore where he first landed (Totnes), was with the People in great jollity and mirth, a crew of these savages, breaking in upon them, began on the sudden another sort of Game than at such a meeting was expected. But at length by many hands overcome, Goemagog, the hugest, in hight twelve cubits, is reserved alive; that with him Corineus, who desired nothing more, might try his strength, whom in a Wrestle the Giant catching aloft, with a terrible hugg broke three of his Ribs: Nevertheless Corineus, enraged, heaving him up by main force, and on his shoulders bearing him to the next high rock, threw him hedlong all shatter'd into the sea, and left his name on the cliff, called ever since Langoemagog, which is to say, the Giant's Leap.

Michael Drayton's Poly-Olbion preserves the tale as well:

Amongst the ragged Cleeves those monstrous giants sought:

Who (of their dreadful kind) t'appal the Trojans brought

Great Gogmagog, an oake that by the roots could teare;

So mighty were (that time) the men who lived there:

But, for the use of armes he did not understand

(Except some rock or tree, that coming next to land,

He raised out of the earth to execute his rage),

He challenge makes for strength, and offereth there his gage,

Which Corin taketh up, to answer by and by,

Upon this sonne of earth his utmost power to try.

Magog in Ireland

"Gog and Magog giving Paddy a Lift Out of the Mire." From Punch magazine, 1849. Here the giants stand for London, said to be assisting Ireland after the famine by purchasing land to improve trade.

Works of Irish mythology, including the Lebor Gabala Erenn (the Book of Invasions), expand on the Genesis account of Magog as the son of Japheth and make him the ancestor to the Irish through Partholon, leader of the first group to colonize Ireland after the Deluge, and a descendant of Magog, as also were the Milesians, the people of the 5th invasion of Ireland. Magog was also the progenitor of the Scythians, as well as of numerous other races across Europe and Central Asia. His three sons were Baath, Jobhath, and Fathochta.[4]

We have shown some extra Biblical mythology, historical, and cultural writings (as done in other areas of this study) because there is so little spoken about Gog—Magog in the Bible. When recorded history and writings of the cultures of others line up in agreement with the Biblical facts and inferences without dispute, they can help color or fill in a clearer picture of a subject.

It is unanimously agreed across the world that Gog—Magog are ferocious and barbaric warriors. In the Bible it says of them:

Amp Ge 10:5 From these the coastland peoples spread.

Much of the mythology and writings about them agree that, they are people of the waters of the oceans—the coastlands even living off fish. Like in the case of Nimrod, they are in some cases thought of to be half-human and half-supernatural, becoming giants. As a result, they are worshiped as the protectors or guardians, or patron demigods (half-human, half-supernatural) of coastal cities such as declared for Britain, Ireland and London, just as in the case of the Philistines.

In addition to being embraced as giants or Nephilim, they are described as hideous, frightening, and animal like, just as the 200,000,000 warriors who come out of the Abyss at the sound of the sixth trumpet. According to their descriptions, it is safe to say Gog—Magog are not a people in the earth today. However, they are associated as living on the edge between the natural realm and the supernatural realm, more specifically, by Hades.

Nimrod, the beast, was the creator of the seven inland empires which were endowed with the powers of the four horsemen. It is easy to glean that Gog—Magog would be the spirit and power behind the coastal empires also endowed and empowered by the power of the four horsemen. Starting with the Phoenicians, and Tyre, up to the modern empires of Britain and Japan to name a few.

In stature, all these mentioned empires are small coastal islands or cities, but through shipping, trade, military strength, and mastery of the seas they became great empires. They are all noted for slave trade or enslavement of people. Because of the many amounts of nations around the world who were conquered into their submission, it was said of the small island of England, "the sun never sets on the British Empire." Meaning, the empire was so global that sunlight would at all times be shining on some of the lands under their control, reflecting that they are from the four corners of the earth. That said, it is important to note that on the future occasion of the end of time, it will be totally comprehensive with participation of all the nations of the globe. That was never achieved before, except when Nimrod will raise from the dead in the future.

In the world, second to only Babylon, is the complete and harsh judgment on the coastal empire Tyre (made great by trade and their mastery of the sea). According to the table of nations in Genesis, Magog was given as his lands and domains, the coastal city of Tyre. It also is important to take note that the Phoenicians, better known as the Philistines, were and are the greatest antagonists of Israel to this day. Going back even further, the Phoenicians were known as Canaanites. However, going forward, the Phoenicians became known as the Philistines and now in modern times, the Palestinians. It was Israel's propensity to worship the gods of the Philistines that became one of their biggest stumbling blocks.

Just as with the seven empires of the beast, it is the spirit power and authority of the four horsemen behind them that all the other coastal empires have risen to their greatness. The total and utter annihilation that was prophesied and happened to Tyre (over centuries), will happen to all the great empires of the coastlands. They are all empowered to be empires by the same power and authority of the four horsemen just as Babylon and its seven empires.

As Nimrod was the human agent of the Devil to give expression to that power, Gog—Magog are the same when it comes to the coastal empires. In fact, they are the patron protectors of England, the greatest of all the coastal empires as far as conquest is concerned. England is where Gog—Magog is celebrated and unwittingly worshiped as its protecting demigod every year to this day.

Through the oceans, these coastal empires ruled and nearly controlled the entire globe—the four corners of the earth—to the degree that "the sun never set on them."

We are told in the Bible that the Devil will go out to deceive the nations in the four corners of the earth to gather them for battle. In their numbers, Gog—Magog, they are like the sands of the sea.

Although the land of Magog is from the Black and Caspian Sea in modern day Russia, the Bible tells us that it is Tyre that Magog was assigned, at the table of nations (Gen 10:1-32). It is not Russia that they will come from when they return, but from Hades in the spiritual realm. That is, if they are not human but supernatural or half-supernatural creatures. Even if where they stream out of the supernatural into the geographic area of Russia by the Black and Caspian Seas, they will not be mortal, nor will they be the mortal people living on earth in submission to the King Christ, in that area of Russia. That is, again, if they are supernatural.

When the Devil was thrown down to the earth and given the key to the Abyss, he let lose unimaginable creatures, which were two of the three woes the world will suffer. Perhaps it is when the Devil is released from the Abyss that he brings with him these creatures called Gog—Magog that help him seduce all the nations except Israel. They could be a great army to serve the Devil and join with human mortals for this endeavor. However, this is speculation based on all the legends and mythologies spoken about Gog—Magog.

In conclusion, it serves best to understand Gog-Magog to be as the Lord speaks of them in Rev 20:7-10: As every nation in the earth and the people in those nations who are the line of offspring of the Devil by choosing to resist the Lord. That would include the supernatural creatures who support them and the Devil. This is the final and ultimate battle which is the fulfillment of the decree the Lord set in motion in the Garden. His purpose is to ensure that not all of humanity would be destroyed, but that those who would reconcile with God, could be saved.

To call the nations Gog-Magog is to understand things through the piercing eyes of God which sees things/people down to their essence from beyond time. Calling them Gog-Magog is to tie this final rebellion of the entire earth against the nation of Israel during their time of favor. This ties the spirit of hatred and murder all the way back to where it began with Nimrod, the table of nations, the Tower of Babel, and the release of the four horsemen. It, likewise, ties it even further back to the Garden, when the Lord decreed an enmity between Eve (the woman clothed with the sun and the crown of twelve stars [the twelve tribes of Israel]) and the offspring of the Devil (all the other nations).

As said previously, when Jesus looked right through Peter's eyes to the essence of the spirit that caused Peter to say what he did, Jesus retorted, "Get behind me, Satan (Mt 16:23)!" Jesus was talking to the essence of the spirit that was behind Peter's words—the very source of them (Satan). By calling the nations Gog-Magog, the Lord is speaking to that army of all the nations (after the 1,000 year reign), piercing through and exposing the very origin of that evil, which is the 70 nations that were spread around the world after the Tower of Babel (except Israel).

Ezekiel prophetically describes the whole event of the battle of Gog and Magog below:

NIV Eze 38:4 *I will turn you around, put hooks in your jaws and bring you out with your whole army—your horses, your horsemen fully armed, and a great horde with large and small shields, all of them brandishing their swords.*

It was said of Nimrod, the beast, that God gave him power to come back from the Abyss because God had put it in his heart to hate the great prostitute. A deal which because of his insatiable lust for power and conquest drew the beast into fulfilling God's own purposes. God is using the unredeemable evil of Gog—Magog in the same way.

NIV Eze 38:5 <u>*Persia, Cush and Put*</u> *will be with them, all with shields and helmets . . .*

These underlined (above) are the lands of Nimrod and Babylon.

NIV Eze 38:6 *also Gomer with all its troops, and Beth Togarmah from the far north with all its troops—the many nations with you.*
NIV Eze 38:7 *" 'Get ready; be prepared, you and all the hordes gathered about you, and take command of them.*
NIV Eze 38:8 *After many days you will be called to arms. In future years you will invade a land that has recovered from war, whose people were gathered from many nations to the mountains*

of Israel, which had long been desolate. They had been brought out from the nations, and now all of them live in safety.

In regard to Israel, Isaiah is speaking about the 1,000 year reign of Christ and how Christ brought all of the Israelites back to the land of Israel with all twelve tribes represented and at peace.

NIV Eze 38:9 You and all your troops and the many nations with you will go up, advancing like a storm; you will be like a cloud covering the land.

NIV Eze 38:10 " 'This is what the Sovereign LORD says: On that day thoughts will come into your mind and you will devise an evil scheme.

NIV Eze 38:11 You will say, "I will invade a land of unwalled villages; I will attack a peaceful and unsuspecting people—all of them living without walls and without gates and bars.

The Lord is talking about the hillsides of Israel during the 1,000 year reign. At this time there is no need for walled cities, because the Lord is there and is their protector.

NIV Eze 38:12 I will plunder and loot and turn my hand against the resettled ruins and the people gathered from the nations, rich in livestock and goods, living at the center of the land."

This is what the nations will say in their hearts about plundering Israel during the 1,000 year reign.

NIV Eze 38:13 Sheba and Dedan and the merchants of Tarshish and all her villages will say to you, "Have you come to plunder? Have you gathered your hordes to loot, to carry off silver and gold, to take away livestock and goods and to seize much plunder?"

NIV Eze 38:14 "Therefore, son of man, prophesy and say to Gog: 'This is what the Sovereign LORD says: In that day, when my people Israel are living in safety, will you not take notice of it?

NIV Eze 38:15 You will come from your place in the far north, you and many nations with you, all of them riding on horses, a great horde, a mighty army.

NIV Eze 38:16 You will advance against my people Israel like a cloud that covers the land. In days to come, O Gog, I will bring you against my land, so that the nations may know me when I show myself holy through you before their eyes.

NIV Eze 38:17 " 'This is what the Sovereign LORD says: Are you not the one I spoke of in former days by my servants the prophets of Israel? At that time they prophesied for years that I would bring you against them.

NIV Eze 38:18 <u>*This is what will happen in that day: When Gog attacks the land of Israel, my hot anger will be aroused, declares the Sovereign LORD.*</u>

NIV Eze 38:19 *In my zeal and fiery wrath I declare that at that time there shall be a great earthquake in the land of Israel.*

NIV Eze 38:20 *The fish of the sea, the birds of the air, the beasts of the field, every creature that moves along the ground, and all the people on the face of the earth will tremble at my presence. The mountains will be overturned, the cliffs will crumble and every wall will fall to the ground.*

NIV Eze 38:21 *I will summon a sword against Gog on all my mountains, declares the Sovereign LORD. Every man's sword will be against his brother.*

NIV Eze 38:22 *I will execute judgment upon him with plague and bloodshed; I will pour down torrents of rain, hailstones and burning sulfur on him and on his troops and on the many nations with him.*

NIV Eze 38:23 *And so I will show my greatness and my holiness, and I will make myself known in the sight of many nations. Then they will know that I am the LORD.'*

NIV Eze 39:1 *"Son of man, prophesy against Gog and say: 'This is what the Sovereign LORD says: I am against you, O Gog, chief prince of Meshech and Tubal.*

NIV Eze 39:2 *I will turn you around and drag you along. I will bring you from the far north and send you against the mountains of Israel.*

NIV Eze 39:3 *Then I will strike your bow from your left hand and make your arrows drop from your right hand.*

NIV Eze 39:4 *On the mountains of Israel you will fall, you and all your troops and the nations with you. I will give you as food to all kinds of carrion birds and to the wild animals*

NIV Eze 39:5 *You will fall in the open field, for I have spoken, declares the Sovereign LORD.*

NIV Eze 39:6 <u>*I will send fire on Magog and on those who live in safety in the coastlands*</u>, *and they will know that I am the LORD.*

The coastlands given to Magog in the table of nations will incur God's wrath is another witness that it is the evil empires which Gog—Magog are demigods over. Even though they will come into the world from the supernatural through a portal from the north in the Caucasus Mountains of the Black Sea. A land they were also Biblically known to occupy.

Note: When Jesus comes at His second coming, the topography of the entire world will change back as it was before the flood. That means that the Caucuses mountain range will be leveled leaving it at best, hills that go up no higher than 12,000 feet. Also, there is one continent and one ocean. Perhaps, that ocean lies to the north and will account for all of the coastal towns that Gog—Magog come from in Ezekiel. However, this is speculation.

NIV Eze 39:7 " *'I will make known my holy name among my people Israel. I will no longer let my holy name be profaned, and the nations will know that I the LORD am the Holy One in Israel.* NIV Eze 39:8 *It is coming! It will surely take place, declares the Sovereign LORD. This is the day I have spoken of.*
NIV Eze 39:9 " *'Then those who live in the towns of Israel will go out and use the weapons for fuel and burn them up—the small and large shields, the bows and arrows, the war clubs and spears. For seven years they will use them for fuel.*
NIV Eze 39:10 *They will not need to gather wood from the fields or cut it from the forests, because they will use the weapons for fuel. And they will plunder those who plundered them and loot those who looted them, declares the Sovereign LORD.*

Many people would not want to give credence to the fact that Gog—Magog is spoken of as using bows and arrows, war clubs and spears, as weapons. They somehow modernize this prophecy because in their minds they think that after all, it is the future . . . there has been great advances in weaponry.

Let's look at the reality of this thinking. First off, it would have been one thousand years of peace because the spirit, power, and authority of conquest and raising armies with the power to kill on a mass scale have been eliminated from the earth. There has been no draft anywhere in the world; no militaries; no military training; no use of any weapons of war; because Jesus is King over the whole world. He peacefully settles disputes among the nations. It also says, that weapon manufacturing has ended, and existing weapons of war have been scrapped and forged into instruments of farming and other tools. Likewise, the time of great manufacturing conglomerates is no more. That way of the world came to an end during the outpouring of God's wrath. That entire system that produced so many tycoons and robber barons is not of God and will be destroyed before Jesus begins His reign.

So, if an uprising were to take place, it makes perfect sense that they would have to construct crude weaponry. There is an almost certain probability King Jesus would not allow the nations the time, resources, and abilities to raise up factories that would mass produce enough weaponry to supply this enormous army. On the other hand, to take pieces of wood and go into the forest and collect wood to make bows and arrows, clubs and spears, would be an easy feat that each individual can do for himself. As such, there is no reason to believe that Ezekiel would be inaccurate simply because he didn't come from a time in which they had weapons of mass destruction.

NIV Eze 39:11 " 'On that day I will give Gog a burial place in Israel, in the valley of those who travel east toward the Sea. It will block the way of travelers, because Gog and all his hordes will be buried there. So it will be called the Valley of Hamon Gog.

NIV Eze 39:12 " 'For seven months the house of Israel will be burying them in order to cleanse the land.

NIV Eze 39:13 All the people of the land will bury them, and the day I am glorified will be a memorable day for them, declares the Sovereign LORD.

NIV Eze 39:14 " 'Men will be regularly employed to cleanse the land. Some will go throughout the land and, in addition to them, others will bury those that remain on the ground. At the end of the seven months they will begin their search.

NIV Eze 39:15 As they go through the land and one of them sees a human bone, he will set up a marker beside it until the gravediggers have buried it in the Valley of Hamon Gog.

NIV Eze 39:16 (Also a town called Hamonah will be there.) And so they will cleanse the land.'

NIV Eze 39:17 "Son of man, this is what the Sovereign LORD says: <u>Call out to every kind of bird and all the wild animals: 'Assemble and come together from all around to the sacrifice I am preparing for you, the great sacrifice on the mountains of Israel. There you will eat flesh and drink blood.</u>

NIV Eze 39:18 <u>You will eat the flesh of mighty men and drink the blood of the princes of the earth as if they were rams and lambs, goats and bulls—all of them fattened animals from Bashan.</u>

The underlined verse above is a judgment/curse upon them which lines up with the suffering of Jesus as He hung upon the cross. He spoke the famous words reciting and fulfilling Psalm 22. The ones heard out loud were:

WEB Ps 22:1 My God, my God, why have you forsaken me?

But later in that Psalm were the words cried out which said:

WEB Ps 22:12 Many bulls have surrounded me.
<u>Strong bulls of Bashan</u> have encircled me.
13 They open their mouths wide against me,

lions tearing prey and roaring.

NIV Eze 39:19 At the sacrifice I am preparing for you, you will eat fat till you are glutted and drink blood till you are drunk.

NIV Eze 39:20 At my table you will eat your fill of horses and riders, mighty men and soldiers of every kind,' declares the Sovereign LORD.
NIV Eze 39:21 "I will display my glory among the nations, and all the nations will see the punishment I inflict and the hand I lay upon them.
NIV Eze 39:22 From that day forward the house of Israel will know that I am the LORD their God.

"From that day forward the house of Israel will know that I am the LORD their God." He is not saying that they did not know that previously. Actually, they will be living in the time of the 1,000 year reign of Christ. What He does mean is that through God destroying the armies of the Devil, Gog-Magog, it is proof absolute that He is the God and protector of Israel. Why is that important? God goes on to explain below. He was always the God and protector of Israel. However, because of their sins and spiritual adulteries, God has used the nations whose gods Israel committed adultery with, to punish them. But at no time were those nations more righteous or more powerful than Israel! God was never too weak to save them from their hands. Nor did the Lord ever love those nations more than Israel because He let them at times dominate them. The Lord explains here (below) in the closing words of what He spoke through Ezekiel that His love for Israel and His promises would never be unfulfilled.

NIV Eze 39:23 And the nations will know that the people of Israel went into exile for their sin, because they were unfaithful to me. So I hid my face from them (desolation) and handed them over to their enemies, and they all fell by the sword.
NIV Eze 39:24 I dealt with them according to their uncleanness and their offenses, and I hid my face from them.
NIV Eze 39:25 "Therefore this is what the Sovereign LORD says: I will now bring Jacob back from captivity and will have compassion on all the people of Israel, and I will be zealous for my holy name.

This here underlined, is one of the great purposes of the thousand year reign of God's Christ. It answers the question: Why is the battle of Gog-Magog is necessary? He will show the whole world, the living and the dead, all of history, that He always loved His people Israel, and never cut them off. But only disciplined them according to their unfaithfulness and according to His perfect justice. He used the sinful nations meant for destruction to be His arm of discipline. However, they were never meant to be cut off and permanently destroyed, never to rise again from their ashes and the smoke of their burning, as the nations of the world have been judged.

Never would God let the nations of His scorn and wrath believe they were righteous over them or that they had a power and authority over them. Or they were in stature elevated above them. This is to show for all time who His love and favor rests upon. Yes, this story has always been about the woman clothed with the sun and the Lord's remnant people gleaned from the twice judged and condemned earth, Israel—the children of His beloved Abraham. Everyone, everything in both the heavens and in the earth for all time will be witness to this faithfulness of God's love and His word.

NIV Eze 39:26 They will forget their shame and all the unfaithfulness they showed toward me when they lived in safety in their land with no one to make them afraid.
NIV Eze 39:27 When I have brought them back from the nations and have gathered them from the countries of their enemies, (for the 1,000 years) I will show myself holy through them in the sight of many nations.
NIV Eze 39:28 Then they will know that I am the LORD their God, for though I sent them into exile among the nations, I will gather them to their own land, not leaving any behind.
NIV Eze 39:29 I will no longer hide my face from them, for I will pour out my Spirit on the house of Israel, declares the Sovereign LORD."

WEB Rev 20:9b Fire came down out of heaven from God, and devoured them. 10 The devil who deceived them was thrown into the lake of fire and sulfur, where the beast and the false prophet are also. They will be tormented day and night forever and ever.

Here we are finally told the end and doom of the Devil! He is to be thrown into the lake of fire just as the beast and the false prophet had. Until the last day, they will be the only occupants in the lake of fire.

Notes

3 *Eschatology.* (n.d.). Retrieved October 2012, from Jewish Encyclopedia: http://www.jewishencyclopedia.com/articles/5849-eschatology
4 *Gog and Magog.* (n.d.). Retrieved August 2013, from Wikipedia, The Free Encyclopedia: http://en.wikipedia.org/wiki/Gog_and_Magog

CHAPTER 6

The Dead are Judged

WEB Rev 20:11 *I saw a great white throne, and him who sat on it, from whose face the earth and the heaven fled away. There was found no place for them.*

Verse 11 (above) brings us to the "last day" or the "day of the Lord." The 1,000 year reign has happened. The last battle of the two different lines of offspring has transpired—the battle of Gog-Magog. The mortal humans of the earth, for the last time, have chosen by which spirit they will be ruled. The choice always remains; to reconcile with God, submitting to His will, and be under His covering, or retain the corrupt human spirit, do your own will and be subject to the Devil. This day is the day of judgment.

Now the Lord has come on His throne, the earth has passed away. In an instant all have died. It is as Peter has told us:

NIV 2Pe 3:5 *But they deliberately forget that long ago by God's word the heavens existed and the earth was formed out of water and by water.*

NIV 2Pe 3:6 *By these waters also the world of that time was deluged and destroyed.*

NIV 2Pe 3:7 *By the same word the present heavens and earth are reserved for fire, being kept for the day of judgment and destruction of ungodly men.*

NIV 2Pe 3:8 *But do not forget this one thing, dear friends: With the Lord a day is like a thousand years, and a thousand years are like a day.*

NIV 2Pe 3:9 *The Lord is not slow in keeping his promise, as some understand slowness. He is patient with you, not wanting anyone to perish, but everyone to come to repentance.*

NIV 2Pe 3:10 But the day of the Lord will come like a thief. The heavens will disappear with a roar; the elements will be destroyed by fire, and the earth and everything in it will be laid bare.

When it says, "everything in it will be laid bare" it means all physical matter will be destroyed. When this happens, every creature with a mortal body made of the elements of the earth will be instantly bodiless, their bodies destroyed along with the earth. Suddenly, with a loud crash, every mortal human will be disembodied—dead, and will have no earth to stand on. Humanity on the earth will be extinct! There will be no more mortal men, ever!

NIV 2Pe 3:11 Since everything will be destroyed in this way, what kind of people ought you to be? You ought to live holy and godly lives
NIV 2Pe 3:12 as you look forward to the day of God and speed its coming. That day will bring about the destruction of the heavens by fire, and the elements will melt in the heat.
NIV 2Pe 3:13 But in keeping with his promise we are looking forward to a new heaven and a new earth, the home of righteousness.

> *WEB Rev 20:12 I saw the dead, the great and the small, standing before the throne, and they opened books. Another book was opened, which is the book of life. The dead were judged out of the things which were written in the books, according to their works. 13 The sea gave up the dead who were in it. Death and Hades gave up the dead who were in them. They were judged, each one according to his works (deeds).*

The entire population of mortal humans on earth stand before the judgment seat of God having been given a resurrected body to do so. Likewise, everyone ever born from the beginning of the earth until the last day, it goes on to tell us, will be given a resurrected body to face the Lord and be judged.

It says the sea gives up its dead. This is very significant, because the sea is the flood waters which destroyed the earth. All who died in the flood will now finally face God and be judged. This verse points out that death and the realm of the dead gave up all its dead and disembodied souls. They too will be given a resurrected body to face the judgment of God.

NIV Mt 10:41 Anyone who receives a prophet because he is a prophet will receive a prophet's reward, and anyone who receives a righteous man because he is a righteous man will receive a righteous man's reward.

NIV Mt 10:42 And if anyone gives even a cup of cold water to one of these little ones because he is my disciple, I tell you the truth, he will certainly not lose his reward."

On this final day of judgment, it is by the lowest standard that the people can be judged as worthy to have eternal life. It is by your deeds while in the body that you are judged on this day. Most all of us suffer death because of the sin of Adam and Eve. The exception being, those who are in union with Christ who never taste death. Through Adam and Eve, death entered into the world. However, it is because we have a just and merciful God that we do rise back to life on the last day. In His total annihilation of the mortal human race he has made a way for each individual who has ever lived to be judged and not condemned because of the sins of others. But by their own conduct.

When I was young and broke the rules by smoking marijuana, each time I saw a policeman, I saw them as a threat to myself and became fearful, even completely self-conscious of how I acted, what I was doing, or what I had to hide from them. However, when I stopped my involvement with marijuana, and after I needed their protection several times, I saw the police in a totally different light. I was most glad that they are there to protect.

The last day of judgment is not something to dread, but an opportunity to be found exempt from the impending death sentence on the human race. It is to be judged on one's own merit and according to his own deeds. Likewise, it will be on one's own merit that he will be condemned to suffer a second death, being thrown alive into the lake of fire. The last day of judgment is a grace and a mercy for those who showed love to their brothers and sisters. To sort out the sheep from the goats and give them pardons, is the reason for the last day of judgment. It is not to search out the guilty, but the innocent. As it was with the flood, the entire human race is condemned again. However, unlike the flood and in keeping with His promises, He will salvage and make celestial humans of those who did good. It is only those who treated their brothers and sisters with evil who will look forward to that day as something terrible.

As such, the last day is to be looked forward to as Peter spoke:

NIV 2Pe 3:11 Since everything will be destroyed in this way, what kind of people ought you to be? You ought to live holy and godly lives

NIV 2Pe 3:12 as you look forward to the day of God and speed its coming. That day will bring about the destruction of the heavens by fire, and the elements will melt in the heat.

NIV 2Pe 3:13 But in keeping with his promise we are looking forward to a new heaven and a new earth, the home of righteousness.

The Sheep and the Goats

NIV Mt 25:31 "When the Son of Man comes in his glory, and all the angels with him, he will sit on his throne in heavenly glory.

NIV Mt 25:32 All the nations will be gathered before him, and he will separate the people one from another as a shepherd separates the sheep from the goats.

NIV Mt 25:33 He will put the sheep on his right and the goats on his left.

NIV Mt 25:34 "Then the King will say to those on his right, 'Come, you who are blessed by my Father; take your inheritance, the kingdom prepared for you since the creation of the world.

NIV Mt 25:35 For I was hungry and you gave me something to eat, I was thirsty and you gave me something to drink, I was a stranger and you invited me in,

NIV Mt 25:36 I needed clothes and you clothed me, I was sick and you looked after me, I was in prison and you came to visit me.'

NIV Mt 25:37 "Then the righteous will answer him, 'Lord, when did we see you hungry and feed you, or thirsty and give you something to drink?

NIV Mt 25:38 When did we see you a stranger and invite you in, or needing clothes and clothe you?

NIV Mt 25:39 When did we see you sick or in prison and go to visit you?'

NIV Mt 25:40 "The King will reply, 'I tell you the truth, whatever you did for one of the least of these brothers of mine, you did for me.'

NIV Mt 25:41 "Then he will say to those on his left, 'Depart from me, you who are cursed, into the eternal fire prepared for the devil and his angels.

NIV Mt 25:42 For I was hungry and you gave me nothing to eat, I was thirsty and you gave me nothing to drink,

NIV Mt 25:43 I was a stranger and you did not invite me in, I needed clothes and you did not clothe me, I was sick and in prison and you did not look after me.'

NIV Mt 25:44 "They also will answer, 'Lord, when did we see you hungry or thirsty or a stranger or needing clothes or sick or in prison, and did not help you?'

NIV Mt 25:45 "He will reply, 'I tell you the truth, whatever you did not do for one of the least of these, you did not do for me.'

NIV Mt 25:46 "Then they will go away to eternal punishment, but the righteous to eternal life.

Note: When Jesus says that when you didn't feed the least of one of these brothers of mine, you didn't feed me . . . it isn't a metaphor, it is literal. Those who are in *spiritual union* with Jesus are one whole person with Him. He died to His body and released His disembodied Spirit to those who would receive it. They died to their lives in the body and instead carry out every prompting of His Spirit. This is *spiritual union* or spiritual marriage and makes true when it is said "and the two shall become one flesh." It also makes it true what Paul said:

Amp Gal 2:20 *I have been crucified with Christ [in Him I have shared His crucifixion]; it is no longer I who live, but Christ (the Messiah) lives in me; and the life I now live in the body I live by faith in (by adherence to and reliance on and complete trust in) the Son of God, Who loved me and gave Himself up for me.*

WEB Rev 20:14 *Death and Hades were thrown into the lake of fire. This is the second death, the lake of fire.* *15* *If anyone was not found written in the book of life, he was cast into the lake of fire.*

There will be no more mortal humans, only celestial humans. The mortal human race will be extinct! Therefore, there will be no more death, accordingly. Death will be thrown into the lake of fire. Hades, the realm of the dead, the prison for the disembodied souls will be emptied at the resurrection after all life has perished. That is, when the earth is thrown into the lake of fire. Hades will have served its purpose and be abandoned. It too will, therefore, be thrown into the lake of fire. Included in Hades will be:

- The paradisiacal place, called Abraham's bosom where those disembodied souls who will be called sheep await the last day, so they may rise and be resurrected.
- The hellish place, where those disembodied souls who will be declared goats on the last day, await the second death while in torment.
- The Abyss, the darkest, deepest bottomless pit of hell where fallen angels, demons, the angels who had mortal women as wives, and the demigods, or giants their union produced, are all imprisoned in the Abyss, along with the most vile of sinners. The Abyss is as Jude describes to us:

NIV Jude 1:4 *For certain men whose condemnation was written about long ago have secretly slipped in among you. They are godless men, who change the grace of our God into a license for immorality and deny Jesus Christ our only Sovereign and Lord.*

NIV Jude 1:5 *Though you already know all this, I want to remind you that the Lord delivered his people out of Egypt, but later destroyed those who did not believe.*

NIV Jude 1:6 <u>*And the angels who did not keep their positions of authority but abandoned their own*</u> <u>*home—these he has kept in darkness, bound with everlasting chains for judgment on the great*</u> <u>*Day.*</u>

NIV Jude 1:7 *In a similar way, Sodom and Gomorrah and the surrounding towns gave themselves up to sexual immorality and perversion. They serve as an example of those who suffer the punishment of eternal fire.*

NIV Jude 1:8 *In the very same way, these dreamers pollute their own bodies, reject authority and slander celestial beings.*

NIV Jude 1:9 *But even the archangel Michael, when he was disputing with the devil about the body of Moses, did not dare to bring a slanderous accusation against him, but said, "The Lord rebuke you!"*

NIV Jude 1:10 *Yet these men speak abusively against whatever they do not understand; and what things they do understand by instinct, like unreasoning animals—these are the very things that destroy them.*

NIV Jude 1:11 *Woe to them! They have taken the way of Cain; they have rushed for profit into Balaam's error; they have been destroyed in Korah's rebellion.*

NIV Jude 1:12 *These men are blemishes at your love feasts, eating with you without the slightest qualm—shepherds who feed only themselves. They are clouds without rain, blown along by the wind; autumn trees, without fruit and uprooted—twice dead.*

NIV Jude 1:13 *They are wild waves of the sea, foaming up their shame; wandering stars, for whom blackest darkness has been reserved forever.*

NIV Jude 1:14 *Enoch, the seventh from Adam, prophesied about these men: "See, the Lord is coming with thousands upon thousands of his holy ones*

NIV Jude 1:15 *to judge everyone, and to convict all the ungodly of all the ungodly acts they have done in the ungodly way, and of all the harsh words ungodly sinners have spoken against him."*

NIV Jude 1:16 *These men are grumblers and faultfinders; they follow their own evil desires; they boast about themselves and flatter others for their own advantage.*

Again, Peter tells us the same:

NIV 2Pe 2:3 *In their greed these teachers will exploit you with stories they have made up. Their condemnation has long been hanging over them, and their destruction has not been sleeping.*

NIV 2Pe 2:4 *For if God did not spare angels when they sinned,* <u>*but sent them to hell, putting them*</u> <u>*into gloomy dungeons* (the Abyss) *to be held for judgment;*</u>

NIV 2Pe 2:5 *if he did not spare the ancient world when he brought the flood on its ungodly people, but protected Noah, a preacher of righteousness, and seven others;*

NIV 2Pe 2:6 *if he condemned the cities of Sodom and Gomorrah by burning them to ashes, and made them an example of what is going to happen to the ungodly;*

NIV 2Pe 2:7 *and if he rescued Lot, a righteous man, who was distressed by the filthy lives of lawless men*

NIV 2Pe 2:8 *(for that righteous man, living among them day after day, was tormented in his righteous soul by the lawless deeds he saw and heard)—*

NIV 2Pe 2:9 *if this is so, then the Lord knows how to rescue godly men from trials and <u>to hold the unrighteous</u>* (in the Abyss) <u>*for the day of judgment, while continuing their punishment.*</u>

The Abyss or bottomless pit, as it is translated sometimes, was meant to imprison celestial beings who have fallen and are deserving of harsh torment, celestial beings who do not die or become disembodied. The Abyss is an especially harsh place for the disembodied souls of men.

WEB Rev 21:1 *I saw a new heaven and a new earth: for the first heaven and the first earth have passed away, and the sea is no more.*

After the great day of the Lord and everyone has been resurrected, faced judgment, and the goats have been thrown alive into the lake of fire to suffer a second death, comes the place reserved for life eternal. The old earth we live in is corrupted and was destroyed. However, God has made a new place! A celestial world even greater than the Garden of Eden

WEB Rev 21:2 *I saw the holy city, New Jerusalem, coming down out of heaven from God, prepared like a bride adorned* (beautifully dressed) *for her husband.*

On that new and uncorrupted earth, the New Jerusalem will rest. It is a city which houses, even clothes the Lord's bride, the celestial humans who ruled with Him during His 1,000 year reign on natural earth.

Note: This reference to the New Jerusalem is after the last day. The New Jerusalem had been on the earth for over 1,000 years during the reign of Christ. The last day came, the earth was destroyed, just as all the physical bodies of the mortal men who were living on the earth when that day came. However, the celestial humans who ruled the earth with the Lord did not die, because their celestial bodies are not made of physical matter. As Jesus promised they are not judged nor do they face the second death. Their place in eternity was secured long before the last day. In fact, they will serve to judge on the last day, testifying either for or against those mortal men who died and are to be resurrected (on the last day) to face judgment.

- Death
- Hades
- The natural earth
- The natural universe
- The fallen celestial beings including the Devil
- The beast and the false prophet
- Those mortal men who were resurrected on the last day and found unworthy to live on for eternity (the goats)

All of which is listed above are thrown into the lake of fire. The only thing which survives the lake of fire on the last day are those who were already celestial humans, the sheep who were found worthy to live on in eternity on the last day, and the New Jerusalem. The New Jerusalem was never a city made of natural matter. Therefore, when the earth, the universe, and all natural matter melts with a sudden and loud crash, it will not affect the New Jerusalem in any form.

The New Jerusalem is a celestial city made of spiritual matter. It had come down from heaven to house the Lord and His ministering celestial humans. It will be ornamented as a bride with all the righteous deeds of those celestial humans who occupy it. Their integrity are the very pillars which hold it up forever, its foundations and gates are the teachings of the 12 Apostles. Its walls that hem in are the purity and faithfulness of the 144,000. Its government will be the celestial humans. It will be presented to the Lord as His bride at its final resting place in the new heavens and the new earth.

> WEB Rev 21:3 *I heard a loud voice out of heaven saying, "Behold, God's dwelling is with people, and he will dwell with them, and they will be his people, and God himself will be with them as their God. 4 He will wipe away from them every tear from their eyes. Death will be no more; neither will there be mourning, nor crying, nor pain, any more. The first things (the old order of things) have passed away."*

When this new heavens and new earth come after the judgment, and the New Jerusalem comes down upon it, the Lord greets all those sheep who on the last day were given celestial bodies and along with it, life eternal. He personally greets and wipes away from each of them, their tears from the pains and hardships of the past when they were mortal humans, and eventually disembodied souls. Once He has done so, they will suffer never again, mourning, crying, nor pain or death. Death will be no more, it will be a thing of the past!

This is the end of the third narrative and it has brought us further into the end of things with more details than in the previous 2 narratives. As such, God Himself concludes this narrative (below) with His promise that this is what awaits all who believe His Son. His Son who is the spirit of prophecy, who was the only one worthy to open the sealed scroll of God's plan for judgment and redemption of the human race. He is the only One who knew its contents and has come clothed like a man to tell us all of what it decreed for the future, and to know how to escape the destruction of the judgment of fire.

Listen with a reverent ear, and hearken to the words of our Creator who speaks tenderly to us now that He has told us His testimony:

> WEB Rev 21:5 *He who sits on the throne said, "Behold, I am making all things new." He said* (to John), *"Write, for these words of God are faithful and true."* 6 *He said to me, "I have become the Alpha and the Omega, the Beginning and the End. I will give freely to him who is thirsty from the spring of the water of life* (all we have to do is want it—to thirst/desire for it). 7 *He who overcomes, I will give him these things* (when the end comes). *I will be his God, and he will be my son.* 8 *But for the cowardly, unbelieving, sinners, abominable, murderers, sexually immoral, sorcerers, idolaters, and all liars, their part is in the lake that burns with fire and sulfur* (when the last day finally arrives), *which is the second death."*

Bibliography

Amplified Bible. Scripture quotations marked (Amp) are taken from the Amplified Bible, Copyright © 1954, 1958, 1962, 1964, 1965, 1987 by The Lockman Foundation. Used by permission.

Ancient Christian Martyrdom. Retrieved June 2018, from *Dallas Baptist University:* *http:*//www3.dbu.edu/mitchell/anceint_christian_martyrdom.htm

Eschatology. (n.d.). Retrieved October 2012, from Jewish Encyclopedia: http://www.jewishencyclopedia.com/articles/5849-eschatology

Gog and Magog. (n.d.). Retrieved August 2013, from Wikipedia, The Free Encyclopedia: http://en.wikipedia.org/wiki/Gog_and_Magog

New International Version. Scriptures taken from the Holy Bible, New International Version®, NIV®. Copyright © 1973, 1978, 1984 by Biblica, Inc.™ Used by permission of Zondervan. All rights reserved worldwide. www.zondervan.com The "NIV" and "New International Version" are trademarks registered in the United States Patent and Trademark Office by Biblica, Inc.™

New Living Translation. Holy Bible, New Living Translation copyright © 1996, 2004, 2007 by Tyndale House Foundation. Used by permission of Tyndale House Publishers Inc., Carol Stream, Illinois 60188. All rights reserved. New Living, NLT, and the New Living Translation logo are registered` trademarks of Tyndale House Publishers.

New Revised Standard Version Bible (NRSV), copyright © 1989 National Council of the Churches of Christ in the United States of America. Used by permission. All rights reserved worldwide.

World English Bible. Scripture quotations marked (WEB) are taken from The World English Bible, which is in the public domain. Special thanks to Michael Paul Johnson and all who worked on the translation as a means to release a modern version of the Bible that is available for non-copyright use. A reminder that the Bible is not owned by man.

Zoller, J. *Pope Gregory VII and King Henry IV.* Retrieved June 2018, from Mr. Zoller's Blog: https://misterzoller.files.wordpress.com/2014/04/popesvskings_henrygregory.pdf

ABOUT THE AUTHORS

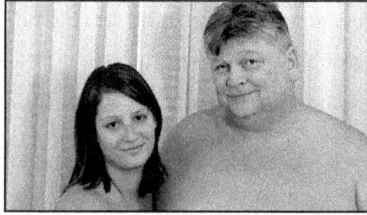

We are just a voice

WEB Jn 1:19 This is John's testimony (about himself), when the Jews sent priests and Levites from Jerusalem to ask him, "Who are you?"
WEB Jn 1:20 He declared, and didn't deny, but he declared, "I am not the Christ."
WEB Jn 1:21 They asked him, "What then? Are you Elijah?"
He said, "I am not."
"Are you the prophet?"
He answered, "No."
WEB Jn 1:22 They said therefore to him, "Who are you? Give us an answer to take back to those who sent us. What do you say about yourself?"
WEB Jn 1:23 He said, "**I am the voice** of one crying in the wilderness, 'Make straight the way of the Lord ...'"

True prophets in the Bible did not convince people who they were; in fact, they refused to talk about themselves. They refused to bring credibility to the words of God they spoke by trying to get people to believe who they were and trust them. They knew that it would be profaning the words of God to do so, and it would be elevating themselves above God's words. They knew that God's words have their own credibility because they are from God. And God will show them (His own words) as from Him.

God's prophets also knew that those who truly love God will, therefore, benefit from their words, and those who are lovers of themselves will not benefit from them, because they will be dismissive and not trust them. The time is over that we look at the person who speaks to decide if we believe. We must begin to discern if the words are from God and if they carry God's Spirit.

You might say to that, "but not everyone can discern God." If that is the case, then they indict themselves as not being "known" by Jesus. They unwittingly reveal about themselves that they desire to do their own will and not the Lord's, just as the religious leaders who wanted Jesus to prove His credibility so they could decide if His words were from God.

Amp Jn 7:16 Jesus answered them by saying, My teaching is not My own, but His Who sent Me. Amp Jn 7:17 If any man desires to do His will (God's pleasure), he will know (have the needed illumination to recognize, and can tell for himself) whether the teaching is from God or whether I am speaking from Myself and of My own accord and on My own authority.

Many will think this is an oversimplified notion. However, it is so simple that it is not only true but reveals a simple but foundational truth about the person. What Jesus is saying is that if a man has a pure heart and wants to do the will of God above his own will, then what seems intuitively right (what sets well with that man) will be God's will and His words. However, even if you are a scholar, theologian, or work in the field of religion, and you desire to carry out your own will, having your own agendas and ambitions, well then, what seems right to that man is not God's will or His words, but that which lines up with his own will.

Generally speaking, the greatest religious minds in the world judge if something is from God by looking at the standing and qualifications of the man speaking them. In the above case, Jesus shows they may be smart in their own eyes, believing they know what is from God and therefore able to judge according to their knowledge of God. However, that would be saying in effect, we know everything about God because of our great knowledge. Therefore, if you say anything outside of our knowledge of God, or outside of the knowledge base of the accepted theological models, or if you are not a qualified student of those accepted models, then we must deduce your words are not from God.

To Jesus, they show about themselves that they don't recognize His words as from God because of their personal acquaintance with God. Instead, they have to judge by facts. They show themselves as having no real relationship with God; they would not recognize Him when He stands right before them. As a matter of fact, on another occasion when they showed contempt for Him, Jesus said of them:

NIV Jn 5:42 ... but I know you. I know that you do not have the love of God in your hearts.

They were once again wanting Him to prove who He was, and what right He had to talk the way He did. Jesus, instead of being intimidated, marveled at how He spoke and acted out everything the Father willed, yet they did not recognize His words as His Father's. Furthermore, they were, by nature, hostile and offended towards those words.

Let's look at that closer through an illustration. For example, you have a woman who claims to be married to a man named Jim. Then, a man claiming to be Jim and her husband approaches her. The above case is like the wife doubting this man is her husband. So then, she begins to question him. For example, "If you're Jim, when were you born?" And, "What kind of car did you have when you first got your license?" If he doesn't answer to her satisfaction, she decides that he is not her husband Jim. This might seem reasonable, and if he got the answers incorrect or didn't remember, the people listening might believe her when she says, "this is not my husband."

If there was anybody in the crowd that had wisdom, they might say this begs another question, "Hey lady, are you really Jim's wife or are you an imposter?" The reasoning of the wise man is, do you really need factual evidence to know if he is your husband? Don't you know your husband when he is standing right in front of you? Jesus is marveling at the religious leaders who are supposed to know God and claim to be in union with Him. However, they don't recognize Him when He stands before them. They don't even recognize His words as from God. Do they really need factual evidence to know something that they are supposed to have intimate knowledge of? Next question, why does it not occur to anyone to question if these men of God, leaders of the Jewish faith, may be imposters because they don't judge if someone and their words are from God by their intimate knowledge of God? They need factual evidence?

What did that tell Jesus? It told Him that even the top religious leaders who know the written word by heart can't recognize God when they stand right in front of Him. It told Him that they were, in their inner man, hostile and threatened by God's words. It told Him that, in their inner selves, they really had no love or even any natural attraction towards God, His heart, and the Spirit of His words. They were obviously naturally repelled by them; they had no real love for God and their response showed it. However, to the religious leaders, they thought themselves wise and discerning to hold Jesus and His words suspect by judging Him with factual evidence. How disappointing it must have been to Jesus that the best of the best had no intimate knowledge of God and they were repulsed by Him when facing Him. Yes, Jesus' deduction was correct, there was no love of God in their hearts.

It is a Biblical fact that the major way we will be judged is it will be proven if we have a natural attraction to please God and do His will, therefore saying about us that we love Him more than ourselves. Learning by the folly of the leaders and the scholarly of Jesus' day, it is not by a knowledgeable and scholarly mind that one can successfully judge or discern what words coming from what person are from God or not. You can't judge superficially. No, it takes something much greater than to know every Bible verse by heart and to be able to have insightful knowledge of the person speaking them. It actually takes something much harder to attain than perfect scholarly knowledge of the written word. It takes a pure heart. Not meaning a sinless heart, but one which is single-minded, wanting to please God by serving Him and wanting to do His will at the expense of their own. This is what qualifies one to recognize if something is from God.

WEB Mt 5:8 Blessed are the pure in heart, for they shall see God.

It is true that as Colleen and I gain a larger following of our teachings and ministry, people will undoubtedly come to know us personally, and what kind of people we are. However, as teachers, we teach people how to live as spiritual men and women, discerning life in a spiritual way.

We have found the best way to teach discerning of spirit. It is not by knowing how to figure people out or to train them to have a spiritual power. No, we teach them to be single-minded when it comes to God, to be surrendered to His will in a pure or holistic way.

Having a still spirit which is not agitated with passions will create a huge contrast. The contrast of having the stillness of God's Spirit rule your heart coming in contact with the agitated spirit energies the people of this world operate out of makes one sensitive to discern spirit.

Jesus was right; wanting to do God's will with all your heart alone will cause you to recognize if one has God's Spirit in them and if they speak word's which are from God. As the saying goes, "You can't cheat an honest man."

NIV Jn 8:15 *You judge by human standards...*

NIV Jn 7:24 *Stop judging by mere appearances, and make a right judgment."*

As such, Colleen and I would like to be known first as a voice, just a voice. We want the words we speak from God to have more prominence and have their own credibility, than that of who we are. Therefore, we don't want to propagate people judging superficially if one is from God by giving our Bio. We want the words we speak to be more important than who we are. We want those who have a pure heart in wanting to serve God to check in their heart if we and the words we speak are from God.

We want those who don't have a pure heart to have a change of heart so they may know for themselves the voice and words of God when they hear them. However, we want to point people in the way to properly discern so they may know for themselves if we are from God and speak His words; in the same way John the Baptist tried to convey. You ask about us, and we will tell you about Him. You insist on wanting to know about us, and we will then tell you, we are just a voice making way for the One you should know and should be asking about. We are not a face or a name or people you should want to know, we are just a voice which gives voice to the One whose words you need to know.

OTHER BOOKS BY THE NAKED APOSTLES

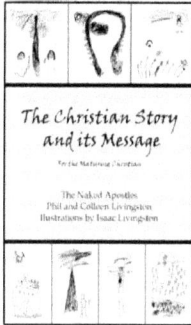

The Christian Story
and its Message

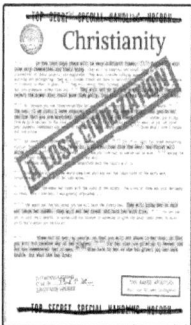

Christianity:
A Lost Civilization

OTHER BOOKS BY THE NAKED APOSTLES

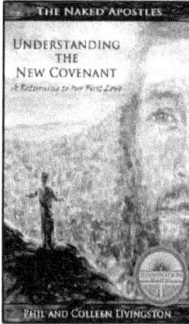

Understanding
the
New Covenant:
*A Returning to Our
First Love*

revelation of Revelation:
*An Urgent Message
for the Church*

Volumes 1-6

For ordering information please visit our website at
www.nakedapostles.org